MALCOLM X

MALCOLM LITTLE

RHYTHM RED

DETROIT RED

SATAN

EL-HAJJ MALIK

EL-SHABAZZ

# MALCOLM X

**HIS LIFE AND LEGACY**

**KEVIN BROWN**

THE MILLBROOK PRESS

BROOKFIELD,
CONNECTICUT

Library of Congress Cataloging-in-Publication Data
Brown, Kevin, 1960–
Malcolm X: his life and legacy/Kevin Brown
p.  cm.
Includes bibliographical references and index.
Summary: A biography of the Nation of Islam's spokesman,
Malcolm X, placed within the context of the civil rights movement.
ISBN 1-56294-500-9
1. X, Malcolm, 1925-1965—Juvenile literature. 2. Black Muslims—
Biography—Juvenile literature. 3. Afro-Americans—Biography—
Juvenile literature. [1. X, Malcolm, 1925-1965. 2. Black Muslims.
3. Afro-Americans—Biography.] I. Title.
BP223.Z8L5724  1995
320.5′4′092—dc20   [B]  94-5381  CIP  AC

Photographs courtesy of UPI/Bettmann: pp. 12, 15, 34, 49, 52, 55, 58
(both) 60, 71, 83, 91, 93, 96; Schomburg Center for Research in Black
Culture, New York Public Library: pp. 17, 20, 23 (photo by Morgan and
Marvin Smith, 1940), 32; The Bettmann Archive: p. 26; Eve Arnold,
Magnum Photos: pp. 29, 39, 74; Robert L. Haggins: pp. 44, 66, 88; John
Launois, Black Star: pp. 47, 85; Russell Shorto, Agincourt Press: p. 100.

Published by The Millbrook Press, Inc.
2 Old New Milford Road, Brookfield, Connecticut 06804

*for Gore Vidal*

*Each one teach on*e.
Black Muslim motto

# CONTENTS

The sudden resurgence of popular interest in Malcolm X a generation after his assassination, particularly among those born after 1965, raises the question: What does he say to young people, all people, today?

American folk heroes as otherwise dissimilar as Malcolm X, Booker T. Washington, Frederick Douglass, Benjamin Franklin, and Abraham Lincoln have this in common: They are quintessentially self-made. The story of Malcolm X is one of transformation and redemption. Without imposing an artificial unity where none exists, I have sketched a portrait that attempts to untangle the thread of Malcolm's various reincarnations from Little to Detroit Red to X to El-Hajj Malik El-Shabazz.

In my research, I have turned inevitably to Alex Haley's *The Autobiography of Malcolm X*. Haley had the first, but by no means the last, word on Malcolm X. For deeper insights, one must turn elsewhere. For, like its subject, the *Autobiography* is a flawed book. Shifting between action and reflection, buoyed by selective surges and lapses of memory as well as a definite political agenda, Malcolm X told an inspired, if not always accurate, story—part sermon, part rap, part monologue.

The present book—part biographical essay and part historical analysis of the Nation of Islam within the larger context of the civil rights movement—draws on a representative cross-section of thinking by writers on Malcolm X. In the end, though, this and all such books can only supplement, not substitute for, *The Autobiography of Malcolm X.*

With the sole exception of Ralph Ellison's *Invisible Man,* there have been few more moving or eloquent testimonials to what Professor Cornel West calls "the sheer absurdity that confronts human beings of African descent in this country."[1] *The Autobiography* is arranged, chapter by chapter, according to each of the phases—gangster, preacher, teacher, martyr—of Malcolm's remarkably varied career. It is a classic of American literature in the great tradition of spiritual and intellectual memoirs such as *Walden, The Education of Henry Adams,* and *The Autobiography of Benjamin Franklin.* In the generation after his assassination, it sold millions of copies. It was as if we looked to it, instinctively, for answers.

I was fifteen when, looking for some answers myself, I first read *The Autobiography of Malcolm X.* Rereading it fifteen years later, I found it even more inspiring. Whatever the final judgment on Malcolm's political and spiritual legacy, he must be recognized for his courage, charisma, and brilliance in struggling to articulate the plight of African Americans and what that bodes for the country at large. To "build on the best of Malcolm X,"[2] as Cornel West put it, we must continue to read, think, and argue about him.

The year 1995, the thirtieth anniversary of Malcolm X's assassination, seems an appropriate time for a biography geared toward young readers either unfamiliar with or looking for a fresh perspective on the subject. And a generation seems sufficient time to reassess, for ourselves and for the future, just what his life has meant. As James Baldwin said, "Our children need both Martin Luther King, Jr., and Malcolm X; and now we . . . must make certain that our children never forget them."[3]

MALCOLM X

Klansmen gather in Alexandria, Virginia, for a cross burning. The man in front is called the Imperial Wizard of the Invisible Empire.

*Still shouting threats, the Klansmen finally spurred their horses and galloped around the house, shattering every windowpane with their gun butts. Then they rode off into the night, their torches flaring, as suddenly as they had come.*[4]

When Malcolm was a young boy, his mother told him this account of how racist violence had threatened the life of his family even before he was born. This heritage of racial violence places him symbolically in a long line of black freedom fighters. It is as if the spirit of martyrdom beckoned to him from the very beginning. "I have never felt that I would live to be an old man," he mused. "Even before I was a Muslim—when I was a hustler in the ghetto . . . [and] in prison, it always stayed on my mind that I would die a violent death." [5]

Religion and politics were the two constants in Malcolm's varied life, and both of these passions were sparked by his father. Though he had finished only fourth grade, Earl "Early" Little was steeped in the ideas of Marcus Aurelius Garvey. A big black one-eyed Georgian, weekdays he was a construction worker. Sundays, Reverend Little was an itinerant preacher, political activist, and organizer for Garvey's Universal Negro Improvement Association (UNIA). Malcolm's father grew his own vegetables, raised his own chickens, and built his own store. Through his father's example, Malcolm X's black nationalism derives more or less directly from Marcus Garvey.

Garvey came to the United States from Jamaica in 1916. Inspired by Booker T. Washington's *Up from Slavery,* he preached economic independence from whites in his weekly newspaper, the *Negro World*. A big black man like Malcolm's father, Garvey wore dazzling, gold-braided uniforms and huge feathered Napoleon hats as he was chauffeured in lavish processions down Fifth Avenue in New York City. Convinced it was hopeless for blacks to expect equality in America, Garvey, an early advocate of black pride, urged them to take the "soul train" back to Africa, land of their forefathers. He even founded a steamship company, the Black Star Line, solely for that purpose.

Garvey's message was a revelation for many like Malcolm, whose idea of Africa was one of "naked savages, cannibals, monkeys, tigers, and steaming jungles." [6] But Garvey's hopes— a new Negro in a new land under a flag of red and black and green—were as outlandish as his schemes. Convicted of swindling his two million supporters out of millions of dollars, Garvey was imprisoned for mail fraud in 1925, the year of Malcolm's birth.

In Omaha, Nebraska, a landmark commemorates the site where Malcolm X was born, on May 19, into a family that would eventually number ten. From Omaha, Earl Little moved his family first to Milwaukee and finally to East Lansing, Michigan. He was "belligerent toward all the children, except me," Malcolm recalled. "I actually believe that, as anti-white as my father was, he was subconsciously so afflicted with the white man's brainwashing of Negroes that he inclined to favor the light ones, and I was his lightest child." [7]

Of all the children, Malcolm alone was allowed to attend UNIA meetings with his father. In East Lansing, as in many

Marcus Garvery, founder of the Universal Negro Improvement Association, in full parade regalia. His espousal of black separatism was the mirror image of the Klan's white supremacist views.

Michigan towns, blacks were forbidden by law to be on the streets after dark. UNIA meetings were necessarily conducted by day, and in secret. Malcolm noticed how different these meetings were from those of his father's congregation. There was none of the jumping or shouting, none of the singing or testifying of the more charismatic black churches. The people seemed "more intense, more intelligent." [8] In their presence he, too, felt more intense, more intelligent. But, for his UNIA activities, Earl Little—four of whose brothers had died violent deaths, including one lynched at the hands of white men—was branded an "uppity nigger." [9]

The last time he saw his father alive, Malcolm was about six. His parents had been fighting. As his father was walking up the road that afternoon after a particularly nasty scene, his mother, who was given to prophetic visions, had the feeling that something terrible was about to happen. "*Early!*" she screamed, running out to the porch after him; but he had already gone. The next anybody saw of him, Earl Little lay bleeding across the streetcar tracks, his head bashed in, his body torn almost in two. The coroner called it an accident. The insurance company claimed suicide. Some said it was murder—most likely by the Black Legion, a Klan-like group that had burned down the Little house two years before.

Louise Little, Malcolm's mother, was a West Indian who looked white. She had, in fact, a white father of whom she was bitterly ashamed. Louise tended to favor the darker children, punishing Malcolm more severely than she otherwise might. Although better educated than her husband, she had no means of supporting the family after her husband's death. Malcolm's older brothers and sisters quietly took on additional responsibilities. But Malcolm began to run wild, fighting with his younger brother at home and with the other boys at school.

It was impossible to make ends meet. Always in the same faded, worn-out dress, with seven children to support, Louise

**Malcolm Little at age fourteen.**

MALCOLM X

**ON CHILDHOOD**

We were so hungry we were dizzy and we had nowhere to turn. Finally the authorities came in and we children were scattered about in different places as public wards. I happened to become the ward of a white couple who ran a correctional school for white boys. This family liked me in the way they liked their house pets.

The *Playboy* interview, May 1963

was weary with washing, cooking, cleaning, fussing. She began to fall into what Earl had always called the "slavery" [10] of debt. Swallowing her pride, she went on relief, enduring abusive social workers in return for packets of meat, potatoes, canned goods, and a meager check. These "homewreckers" [11] assumed the right to treat her family as they saw fit, coming around, asking questions, turning the children against her and against each other. Bad got worse during the Depression of the 1930s. Dizzy with hunger, Malcolm and his brothers supplemented the dandelion greens that grew wild along the roadside with whatever they could steal. His life of crime had already begun.

Bitter and resentful, Louise began to lose touch with reality. She was found wandering in the snow on Christmas morning, barefoot and dirty, in her arms an illegitimate child, her eighth. Louise Little was put in a mental institution, where she languished for twenty-six years. Malcolm was sent first to a foster home, and then to a detention home in the small town of Mason, Michigan. He was thirteen.

Later, at mostly white Mason Junior High, Malcolm was popular, but bright enough to resent being a token black. He loved to learn, though, especially history. Mathematics left no room for argument: you were either right or wrong. Not so with history, where there was room for debate. Malcolm found he had a taste for argument. But he was in for a shock: The section on Negroes in his history text was exactly one paragraph long.

In eighth grade, Malcolm told one of his teachers that he hoped to become a lawyer. With good intentions, Malcolm was advised that, being black, he should set his sights on a more realistic goal like carpentry. For the first time, Malcolm began to feel bored and dissatisfied, with Mason and with white people. That summer, when school was out, Malcolm boarded a Greyhound bus and went to live with his half-sister in Boston, never to return to Mason or to formal schooling again.

18

# REBELLION

Boston was bewildering. Malcolm stood on the Common, gawking at the statue of Crispus Attucks, the first man killed in the Boston Massacre of 1770. Crispus Attucks was black. Malcolm's history paragraph had neglected to mention that. The Bostonians were bewildering, with their worldly talk and worldly ways. As casually as they might mention neighboring small towns, people dropped the names of—had actually been to—famous cities like New York and Chicago.

Malcolm ventured out into the streets of Roxbury, black Boston, with its pool halls, juke joints, and two-dollar prostitutes. He never dreamed the world contained such varieties of black people. Suddenly, he became aware of differences not just between but within the races. Native-born African Americans had a slur for West Indians: "black Jews."[12] So-called professional Negroes—teachers, preachers, mailmen, Pullman porters—considered themselves superior to common blacks. In East Lansing the only "successful" Negroes had been janitors, country club waiters, or state capitol shoeshine boys. But even in Boston it didn't escape Malcolm's notice that the only Negroes with any real money, whatever their social status, were pimps and racketeers.

Rhythm Red, zoot-suited and streetwise, after his move to the Roxbury section of Boston at age fifteen.

For it was 1940, and though the Great Depression was past, the boom years of World War II were yet to come. Malcolm looked twenty-one but wasn't quite sixteen. He found himself a "slave," a job shining shoes at the Roseland State Ballroom, popping the shoeshine rag like a firecracker for the smug satisfaction of white customers who sat in his chair before the Benny Goodman, Duke Ellington, or Count Basie big bands went on at eight o'clock. Beyond a spitshine, Malcolm quickly learned to provide some reefer, a little bootleg liquor, or whatever else his well-heeled clientele might require.

He had come to Boston a country bumpkin in highwater pants. Now, zoot-suited in Easter bunny colors and orange shoes, his hair conked, Rhythm Red was himself a hipster, lindy-hopping at Roseland on his days off. Cursing came as naturally as speaking. Running with an older, faster crowd, chain-smoking four packs of cigarettes a day, Malcolm shot his first craps, played his first number, had his first drink, and smoked his first reefer.

Once he got the feel of Boston, Malcolm became a Pullman porter. He had always dreamed of seeing what the musicians, traveling salesmen, chauffeurs, and petty hustlers called the Big Apple—especially Harlem. And so, every other day for four hours, he bellowed up and down the aisles, hawking railroad commissary on the Boston–New York run of the *Yankee Clipper*.

"New York," he said, "was heaven to me. And Harlem was Seventh Heaven!" [13] In black Manhattan, across 110th Street, there were the Savoy Ballroom, Apollo Theater, Hotel Theresa, and the Braddock, whose bar was famous as a jazz hangout. On any given night, you could walk in and see Dizzy Gillespie, Billy Eckstine, Ella Fitzgerald, or Dinah Washington. And at 4 A.M., when "legit" joints closed, after-hours spots kept jumping well into the next day. "Within the first five minutes," Malcolm remembered, "I had left Boston and Roxbury forever." [14]

**ON HARLEM**

That's where I saw in the bars all these men and women with what looked like the easiest life in the world. Plenty of money, big cars, all of it. I could tell they were in the rackets and vice. I hung around these bars whenever I came in town, and I kept my ears open and my mouth shut. And they kept their eyes on me, too. Finally, one day a numbers man told me that he needed a runner, and I never caught the night train back to Boston.

The *Playboy* interview,
May 1963

At first, gradually transplanting himself from Boston, Malcolm stayed at the 135th Street YMCA. Then he rented a room in a nearby boardinghouse. Venturing from the stolid, well-lit streets of Sugar Hill and into the raucous avenues, Malcolm found the overflowing garbage cans, winos and junkies, pawnshops and barber shops, beauty parlors and funeral parlors, and storefront gospel churches of down-home Harlem. Or he traveled downtown to the white neighborhoods of what he called "swank brownstones and exclusive apartment houses, with doormen dressed like admirals." [15]

Already a hanger-on and dealer to famous musicians, exchanging profane pleasantries with Billie Holiday at Small's Paradise, Malcolm now sold reefer like a wild man, enjoying secondhand the glamour and prestige of celebrityhood. "Almost everyone in Harlem needed some kind of hustle to survive," Malcolm explained, "and needed to stay high in some way to forget what they had to do to survive." [16] Up and down the East Coast, along the route he had previously traveled as a Pullman porter and would later travel as an itinerant preacher, he followed jazz bands from town to town.

Among gangsters as among jazz musicians, a nickname was a badge of honor. Malcolm's reputation soon spread through the grapevine. Because he was from Michigan, and because of his reddish complexion, he was dubbed Detroit Red. From bootlegging, numbers running, and drug dealing, the eighth-grade dropout quickly graduated to armed robbery. "I carried not *a* gun," he confessed, "but *some* guns." [17] He believed "a man should do anything that he was slick enough, or bad and bold enough, to do." [18] But the paranoia and jitters from five years of hustling and drug addiction finally caught up with him.

Harlem turned out to be a dead end. In his last days, a desperado running from one dingy furnished room to another, living stickup to stickup, staying high to keep from falling prey to fear and self-contempt, Malcolm was, he knew, "walking on

Dancing at the Savoy, which Lana Turner nick-named the Home of the Happy Feet. Detroit Red got caught up in the swirl of 1940s Harlem until the dream turned to nightmare.

my own coffin."[19] Finally, busted for possession of stolen property, Malcolm was convicted and sentenced to ten years. He felt he'd "sunk to the very bottom of the American white man's society." It was in prison, ironically, that he would be set free. There, "I found Allah and the religion of Islam, and it completely transformed my life." [20]

**THE WORDS**

Charlestown State Prison was almost medieval. The cells were cold, cramped, and filthy, with no running water and only covered pails for toilets. Deprived of drugs and miserable, Malcolm actually preferred solitary confinement, where for hours he paced like a caged animal, cursing God and man. He was so mean the other inmates soon had their own nickname for him: Satan.

After a year, Malcolm was transferred to Concord, Massachusetts, where in a letter he learned of something his brother Philbert called the Nation of Islam, "the natural religion for the black man." [21] Rolling his eyes, Malcolm paid it no mind. Philbert was always joining something. First it was the Holiness Church, now this. Then he learned that not only Philbert but all his brothers and sisters had converted to this new faith. They advised him to give up pork and cigarettes, promising to show him a way out of prison. That got his attention. Naturally, the hustler assumed his family had figured out some parole board scheme. He began corresponding with his brothers and sisters, learning more about the teachings of Elijah Muhammad.

Letter writing was Malcolm's most immediate way of improving his education. On the street, he had been the most articulate of con men. In prison, he found himself functionally

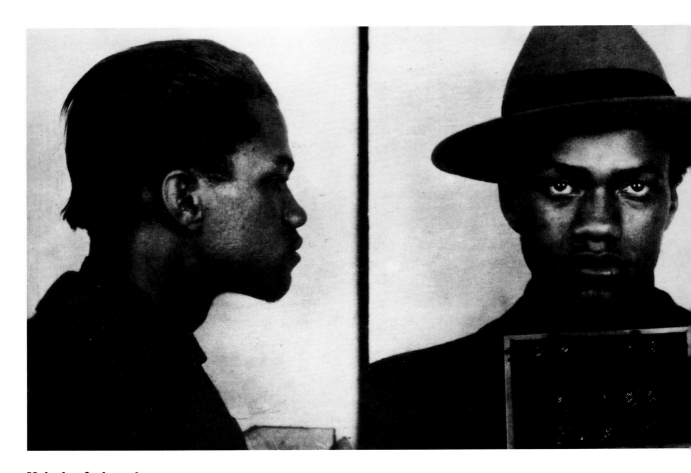

**Malcolm, facing a ten-year prison term at age twenty-one. The intensity of his rage led inmates to call him Satan.**

illiterate. "Every word I spoke was hip or profane. I would bet that my working vocabulary wasn't two hundred words." [22] His grammar was poor, his penmanship worse. He knew what he wanted to say, but was unable to say it. It was rough at first, but after a year or so he could compose a decent letter.

Malcolm's sister Hilda challenged him to his first test. He was to write a letter in perfect English, in care of Elijah Muhammad in Chicago, to his savior and deliverer Allah. He was to swear that he had studied, believed, and bore witness to the teachings, that there was no God but Allah, and that His apostle was Elijah Muhammad. He was also to request his Original Name, to be exchanged at some later date for his "slave name." In fact, Malcolm wrote petitioning the governor, the president—everybody.

Only Elijah Muhammad answered. He told Malcolm that the white man, systematically whitewashing history, had maliciously distorted the record of the black man's achievement, teaching that he had no culture, no civilization. Elijah Muhammad, on the other hand, preached black pride. He taught that blacks were in fact the heirs of ancient kings and kingdoms in Ethiopia and West Africa, which, while Europeans were savages still living in caves and painting themselves blue, had enjoyed the benefits of science and technology. He said that black, which contains all colors, was perfect; and white, the absence of color, defective. The white race, he said, was the result of a mad experiment by a black scientist, Yacub, who had rebelled against Allah. The white man, a devil by nature treacherous and immoral, had ruled the world for six thousand years, but would, he swore, be overthrown in the coming battle of Armageddon.

Christianity, according to Elijah Muhammad, was the white man's religion—a tool to keep the black man down. The greatest crime in human history was the European murder, rape, pillage, and enslavement of African and other nonwhite civilizations. And, ultimately, blacks in prison were the white man's burden, he said. Had he not first enslaved and then oppressed them, denying them opportunities for decent education and employment, they would never have turned to crime in the first place. Elijah Muhammad assured Malcolm that he understood completely; for he himself had once languished in the white man's prison.

It sounded crazy at first: the white man a *devil*? Malcolm searched his past, thinking of all the whites he had ever known. Bitterly, he remembered the loss of his father, the welfare workers, his dreams dashed in school, and now the brutal prison guards. Still skeptical, he sought proof of Elijah Muhammad's teachings. In March 1948, Malcolm had been transferred again, this time to Norfolk, an experimental rehabilitation center in the country with fresh air, running water, flushing toilets, and no cell bars, violence, rape, or official brutality. He had his own room and, best of all, in a library stocked with thousands of books, complete freedom of the shelves. The books in the prison library, however, might as well have been in Greek, for all the words he failed to recognize. And skipping words made the books incomprehensible. He could only go through the motions. Frustrated, from the prison classroom Malcolm requested pencils, paper, and, most important, a dictionary.

"I spent two days just riffling through the dictionary . . . . I'd never realized so many words existed! I didn't know *which* words I needed to learn. Finally . . . I began copying." [23] His handwriting began to improve as, page by page, Malcolm copied the dictionary. Words, words he had never even imagined came to life, weird words like *aardvark*. The words had pictures, and the pictures had connections to people, places, and things in a vaster world than he'd ever dreamed of. A book of words, the dictionary seemed to contain the roots of all knowledge.

Words begot words, and those words begot books. At first indiscriminately and without guidance, later selectively and

**Elijah Muhammad, leader of the Nation of Islam and mentor to Malcolm X, who worshiped him.**

more focused, Malcolm devoured history, religion, and philosophy: H.G. Wells's *Outline of History*, Milton's *Paradise Lost*, W.E.B. Du Bois's *Souls of Black Folk*; Confucius and Eastern philosophy; the Western philosophies of Kant, Schopenhauer, and Nietzsche; Louis Leakey, the anthropologist who claimed, on the basis of fossils found in Kenya, that all mankind originated in Africa one million years before the birth of Christ—he read them all.

The Roman Empire, an ancient multiracial world that stretched from the Middle East to North Africa and up through Europe, fascinated him. The African-American slave rebellions, when Nat Turner and scores of fugitives ran amok slaughtering slave masters in the night and eluding federal soldiers for months, amazed him. The British occupation of China, her population demoralized with opium, enraged him. The famous African tribes—Ashanti, Masai, Yoruba, and Zulu—inspired him. This was Malcolm's first, most profound, and, in the end, most lasting conversion: to words, books, and ideas. This was the one that would sustain him when all else failed.

"It was a revelation, like a blinding light."[24] Malcolm became a true believer, seeing in Elijah Muhammad both a black Messiah and a father figure. Unable to eat for long periods, he sat and stared into space, or else admired photographs of the Messenger. He studied that kindly face, the nut-brown complexion, the delicate features framed by the fez of golden thread, until he saw it in his dreams. But belief was one thing; submission and prayer on bended knees was quite another. That would take some doing. Feeling foolish at first, he tried. He failed. He tried again. Gradually, "my previous life's thinking pattern slid away from me, like snow off a roof." [25] He praised Allah for His benevolence.

Simplistic as it sounds, Elijah Muhammad's dogma was what Malcolm came to believe. His lack of formal education blinded him to what was fact and what fiction. True, Aesop, author of the Greek fables, was black. True, there was once a great university at Timbuktu in West Africa, long before Harvard and Yale. However, that history was known in advance by a council of twenty-four black scientists, with a twenty-fifth serving as chief justice, was far-fetched. That the black man was the Original Man, descended from the tribe of Shabazz sixty-six trillion years ago, was absurd. And that all Malcolm's years hustling on the streets hadn't taught him whites had no monopoly on evil is sad. At once cynical and naive, Malcolm was formed in a world that had stripped him of belief, but not the need to believe. Rejected and rejecting, he felt he had found at last in the Nation of Islam what he'd missed growing up in a broken home and a racist society: a sense of self, the promise of a new life, and a faith by which to live.

Secluded from the other inmates, Malcolm devoted almost every waking moment to study. "The ability to read awoke in me some long-dormant craving to be mentally alive." [26] Whole days of as many as fifteen hours were consumed in reading hundreds of books. At night, after lights out, every hour on the hour when the guard's footsteps echoed down the sleeping corridor, Malcolm hopped back into his bunk, pretending to be asleep. Once the guard left, he crawled back to the floor for another fifty-eight minutes in order to read in the faint glow of a night light until three or four o'clock in the morning.

Years later, at Oxford and other universities, Malcolm would say by way of introduction that he had finished eighth grade, graduated from high school in the ghetto of Boston, earned his bachelor's degree hustling the streets of Harlem, and taken his master's in the prison library. His prison years were indeed the most intellectually productive of his life. "Between Mr. Muhammad's teachings, my correspondence, my visitors . . . and my reading . . . months passed without my even thinking about being imprisoned. In fact, up to then, I had never been so truly free in my life." [27]

**ON FAITH**

A new world order is in the making, and it is up to us to prepare ourselves that we may take our rightful place in it.

Epistle to one of the Nation of Islam brethren

**Malcolm X, transformed.**

To test his wits, Malcolm entered the prison debating society. He spent hours preparing, strategizing, putting himself in his opponent's place, anticipating arguments. Which side he was on hardly mattered. It was the hunt for ideas and arguments, followed by the kill on the debating floor with a devastating twist of logic, that thrilled him. He loved words and arguments. He felt he might have been a lawyer—anything. And just as when, a small boy of eight or nine, he had lain on a hill behind the house in East Lansing to look up at the sky and dream, so now, lying on his bunk in the dark solitude of his cell, he imagined himself preaching to the multitudes. "It was right there in prison that I made up my mind to devote the rest of my life to telling the white man about himself—or die." [28]

Malcolm Little had served six and a half years when the Massachusetts State Parole Board voted his release in 1952. On the outside, almost as if he knew he hadn't much time left, the first thing he purchased with his new freedom was a watch. He had entered prison conked, subliterate, hostile; he emerged bookish, bespectacled, his hair close-cropped and kinky. He had changed his values, speech, and religion, and soon he would even change his name. He had made sacrifices. His redemption had not been easy, but it had been glorious. He had acquired that most important possession: self-respect. He was further strengthened in the knowledge that he was no longer alone but part of a growing Nation, heir to the power and the glory of Africa's imperial past. Now he knew the truth, and the truth had set him free.

**Muhammad speaks at a Black Muslim convention in Chicago, heavily guarded by the Fruit of Islam, a paramilitary unit uniformed in conservative suits and ties, white shirts, and close-cropped hair.**

# MUHAMMAD SPEAKS

Upon his release from prison in 1952, Malcolm went to live not in Boston or Harlem but at his brother's home in Detroit. There, he found the stability of Muslim ritual and family life. In the morning, there was the bathing, grooming, and greeting: *As-Salaam-Alaikum* ("peace be unto you"); *Wa-Alaikum-Salaam* ("and peace be unto you"). Evenings, when the sun was low on the horizon, on a rug devoted solely to that purpose, there was prayer to Allah, facing east in a gesture of unity with Muslims everywhere, eyes open so as not to lose sight of His creation, palms face up and cupped as if to catch His blessings. In between, at noon and again at three, there was daily meditation, *Allahu-Akbar, Allahu-Akbar* ("Allah is greatest"), chanted softly to oneself.

One Sunday, Malcolm made a pilgrimage to hear Elijah Muhammad speak at one of the Nation's legendary rallies in Chicago. Following Muhammad's police-escorted motorcade, hundreds of chartered buses converged on the Coliseum. At the doors and onstage, stern-faced, sober-suited guards patrolled with military deportment, walkie-talkies in hand, searching visitors for alcohol, tobacco, or firearms and lending the whole event an air of excitement and even danger. And, for once, the tables were turned: Whites were strictly forbidden.

There was a brief calm before the storm of applause as Elijah Muhammad walked to the lectern and greeted the crowd. For two or three hours, despite convulsive fits of coughing, he heaped scorn upon the white man. The audience was attentive, the atmosphere intense. There was no singing or dancing. The so-called Negro, Muhammad said, had already done too much singing and dancing for the white man's entertainment. Only here and there the occasional affirmation was audible: "That's right! Preach!" Tears welled up in Malcolm's eyes. He could *feel* the power—as if he were witnessing firsthand the presence of Allah. Suddenly, out of the blue, the Messenger called his name, singling him out before the audience as living proof of Allah's power to change lives. "It was," Malcolm remembered, "like an electrical shock." [29]

Ominously, even at that first rally, vicious rumors about Elijah Muhammad reached Malcolm's ears. His own brother Reginald hinted darkly about Muhammad's private life. Others were suspicious of his move into an eighteen-room mansion in Chicago. Malcolm refused to listen.

"Go after the young people." [30] For Malcolm, the Messenger's words carried the force of commandment. Fired up from the rally, he approached the minister of Detroit's Temple No. 1 and offered his services. The more complacent view of some was that Allah would bring converts into the fold as He saw fit. Not content to sit around and wait for the Nation's ranks to swell through word of mouth, Malcolm urged an aggressive recruitment campaign. Harlem, Boston, Detroit—it hardly mattered. He knew how best to reach the ghetto, understood its thinking, spoke its language. The minister agreed.

From that day on, Malcolm went door to door wherever black people congregated—in living rooms, storefronts, pool halls, on idle street corners—"fishing" for lost souls. Churches were outnumbered only by liquor stores in vying for a share of the misery market. The Messenger encouraged his fishermen to trawl the murky ghetto bottom. Ex-cons and reformed addicts often made the best converts. Polite, well dressed, soft-spoken, and self-assured, these recruits in turn recruited others for "manhood training," vividly demonstrating how someone once like them—hungry, scratchy, smelly—could command respect with self-respect. Malcolm regarded himself as proof that there was no reform like that which came from below.

Soon after the rally, Malcolm Little received from Chicago the name by which he would be known to history. He shed his "slave name" and became Malcolm X—"X" as in "ex-," "X" as in unknown, symbolic of the identity stripped from him, as from millions of slaves in centuries past.

Within a few months, Temple No. 1 tripled its membership. "And that so deeply pleased Mr. Muhammad," Malcolm recalled, "that he paid us the honor of a personal visit." [31] Elijah Muhammad took note of his new disciple. He could see that this Malcolm X was sharp, could think on his feet. Malcolm, for his part, worshiped the Messenger. He found in Muhammad the living practice of what his father had died preaching. Like Marcus Garvey, Elijah Muhammad seemed like a black Moses leading his people out of bondage through the wilderness of North America.

Malcolm was invited to address the Detroit temple. His previous public-speaking experience had been confined to prison debates. Malcolm discovered he loved the limelight. Not since his father's UNIA meetings had he felt such a spine-tingling *thrill*. Sometimes his eyes welled up with tears, he was so bitter and angry about what he was saying. Immediately, he was hooked. He spoke so often he stayed hoarse. He could hardly wait for the next time all eyes would look up to him standing tall at the lectern, saying, "I have pledged on my knees to Allah to tell the white man about his crimes and the black man the true teachings of our Honorable Elijah Muhammad. I don't care if it costs my life." [32]

Already Assistant Minister of Temple No. 1, Malcolm journeyed to Chicago as often as he could, at the Messenger's encouragement. Like Malcolm's father, Elijah Muhammad was a Georgian with only a fourth-grade education. Slight, frail, and asthmatic, he wore dark suits and bow ties capped off with a distinctive star-and-crescent pillbox hat. His oddly dainty manner, however, could not conceal the deadly determination in those penetrating eyes and thin mouth. Briskly energetic, he worked eighteen-hour days, dining only once, at 6:00 P.M. In public, Elijah Muhammad was solemn, intense, fanatical. But this hostility was purely professional. In private, at his national headquarters, there were no bodyguards. In private, he was gracious, soft-spoken. In private, he preached not hatred but enterprise. Muhammad treated Malcolm like a son, advising him on the best way to spread the message. And it was during these visits that Malcolm learned about the life of the Messenger and his movement.

Born Elijah Poole in 1897 at Sandersville, Georgia, he was one of thirteen children. Like his father before him, he became a preacher. During his twenties, Elijah moved to Detroit, where the effects of the Depression on the ghetto had been devastating. Instead of the promised land, he found only police brutality, overcrowded slums, dead-end jobs, and rude welfare workers.

During the early 1930s, Elijah was visited by one Master Fard. He had come, it was said, from the Holy City of Mecca to prepare his people for Armageddon—the ultimate battle between black and white, good and evil. A door-to-door proselytizer claiming to have been entrusted with the spiritual care and guidance of African Americans, Fard converted thousands. God, he taught, was only another name for Allah. Islam was the true religion, and Muslims were God's chosen people. And since blacks were not given the same protections and guarantees as other Americans, they owed no allegiance to America or its flag.

Malcolm X with Elijah Muhammad. "My worship of him was so awesome," said Malcolm, "that he was the first man whom I had ever feared—not fear such as of a man with a gun, but the fear such as one has of the power of the sun." (*The Autobiography*)

39

If they could not receive justice or equality within the United States, they should establish a nation of their own. Thus was born the Nation of Islam, with its professed aim of establishing an economically and politically separate state or territory, either in America or abroad.

The first Black Muslim mosques were abandoned churches, synagogues, or even funeral parlors. Run on shoestring budgets, these temples stayed close to the ghetto, the better to reach potential converts. The membership, consisting of ex-cons, recovering addicts, and reformed prostitutes, was largely illiterate and poor.

Founded in 1931 by Master Fard, tiny Detroit Temple No. 1 (the temples were numbered until this was found to be a convenient way for the FBI to count the strength of the movement) was the very first Black Muslim mosque. Inside, as a reminder to its members of their condition in American society, was a blackboard painted in indelible red, white, and blue with the Stars and Stripes, below it the words "Slavery, Suffering and Death." Painted next to the flag was a cross, beneath it the word "Christianity," and on the cross, a dangling man—lynched at the hands of hooded Klansmen.

Persecuted and arrested, Fard was sent to prison. Released two years later, in 1934, Fard disappeared as mysteriously as he had come. Some said he had been murdered, others that he had gone back to Mecca. Fard was later made out to be far more than a prophet. He was proclaimed none other than Allah in the flesh.

Fard had raised Elijah Poole from the gutter. A dedicated member of the movement, he had been to Fard what Malcolm would later be to him: his single most diligent and trusted servant. In 1933, Elijah established a temple on the South Side of Chicago. It soon got about that Elijah, too, was divinely inspired, sent by Allah to fulfill the prophecy of Fard. Elijah Poole was rechristened Elijah Muhammad ("one worthy of praise"). He had transformed himself first into Fard's lieutenant, then into "the Honorable Elijah Muhammad," and ultimately into the Messenger of Allah himself.

During World War II, Elijah Muhammad was arrested by the FBI and sentenced to five years in a federal prison for draft dodging and publicly sympathizing with the Japanese. Too old for military service, he was, in his own mind, a political prisoner. Besides, since blacks were denied full rights of citizenship, what was there to fight for? Having served three and a half years, Elijah Muhammad was released from prison and returned to rule the emerging Nation in 1946, the same year Malcolm was sentenced.

Black history has had more brilliant thinkers than Elijah Muhammad, but perhaps never a shrewder psychologist. The secret of great leadership, he sensed, was knowing where followers wanted to be led. African Americans, he reasoned, had a ready-made cause. All they needed was a leader. He surrounded himself with a band of handpicked devotees, the faithful's faithful, who both obeyed without question and were themselves effective leaders, Malcolm most of all. Muhammad must have known what he meant to Malcolm, as he had to many another convict cut off from society, family, and friends, to whom a sympathetic letter and a little commissary money meant more than anything in the world. Muhammad must have known, as Garvey had known, what the stylized rituals—the uniform dress code, the long bus caravans headed to distant rallies of the faithful, all the regalia of belonging—meant to many a fatherless child. Symbol clad, he inspired their devotion. Velvet gloved, he wielded iron-fisted control. Uneducated he might be; unknowing he certainly was not.

The press, he gloated, completely failed to grasp this. They called him a fake, a hatemonger. The press might not endorse him, but even negative publicity was better than no publicity at all. The papers, he knew, existed to sell news. And he was news. Black businessmen might not buy his theology, but they certainly valued his "buy black" economics, not to mention the fact that the Nation of Islam paid its bills on time and in cash. He was not learned like Malcolm, he could admit it. Uncle Tom intellectuals, with their Ivy League pedigrees, ridiculed him, but they might listen to Brother Malcolm. Still, for all their knowledge, they lacked understanding. Authenticity was irrelevant; even truth was irrelevant. The Muslims followed him not for his ideas but for his inspiration, not for his symbols but for the certainty they conveyed. Belief and the will to believe were all.

As for hatred, that was his most potent weapon. Whatever the differences among blacks, they were alike discriminated against. Even more than the Muslims' love of Allah, it was their common hatred of the blue-eyed devil that united them. And the devil was visible everywhere you looked. All failures were due to him, and all victories triumphs over him. As for Christianity, the white man's religion, even he did not believe in it, if his behavior was any indication.

Muhammad saw himself as a champion of the true religion in the face of a false god. And so, patient with the enemy, assured as if he possessed hidden knowledge concerning the outcome of the battle between good and evil and the ultimate victory of his crusade, His Mysteryship Elijah Muhammad smiled that enigmatic smile, serene in the certainty that the black Nation would someday inherit the Earth.

Minister Malcolm X became a traveling missionary, establishing fledgling temples from town to town all across the country. "A ghetto street hustler turned grimly austere evangelist," [33] as one writer put, he excoriated the blue-eyed devil—eloquently. Controversy piqued interest. The curious, once inside, were hooked. Those who heard the fiery minister returned, bringing others. So spread the word, in a groundswell of enthusiasm, outrage, or mere curiosity. But in those early years, though many believed, few followed. The Muslims' forbidding austerity concerning almost every pleasure life afforded—pork, tobacco, alcohol, singing, gambling, movies, makeup, dating, dancing, extramarital sex, and even sports—made the Nation of Islam a hard sell in the black community.

About this time, Malcolm began to attract attention from a different quarter. The FBI began paying him little visits, at first fearing he might be a Communist sympathizer, and later that he might be a militant agitator. Didn't he know there was a war on with Korea? Why hadn't he registered for the draft? Malcolm explained that, as a Muslim, he was a conscientious objector. Did he have any idea, they sneered, just what the words "conscientious objector" meant? Malcolm shot back that the idea of dying to preserve a way of life that denied black Americans their civil rights demanded that his conscience object.

New York City, with a black population of over one million, was of obvious strategic importance to the Nation. In 1954, Malcolm was made minister of Temple No. 7, on the corner of 116th Street and what is now Malcolm X Boulevard. The number of Black Muslims in the whole of New York City being less than a busload, the mosque was little more than a storefront. Gradually, meeting by meeting, every Sunday at 2:00 P.M. and again on Wednesdays and Fridays at 8:00 P.M., the mosque grew. But Malcolm was never satisfied. Scorning what he saw as the complacency of more conservative ministers, he was eager for the Nation to grow—faster. On one of Malcolm's visits to Chicago, Elijah Muhammad warned him, cryptically, "I would rather have a mule I can depend upon than a racehorse I can't."[34] Character, said the ancient Greek philosopher Heracleitus, is fate. Long and lean, Malcolm was a racehorse, not a mule. He was built for speed, not endurance.

Nevertheless, knowing how he hated to be tied down, how he longed to be out and about, "fishing" in far-off cities, Muhammad bought Malcolm a brand-new car. Word on the street was that Detroit Red was on some religious kick. His homeboys

Minister Malcolm X speaks at a Harlem rally. "His moral force," said his close friend Dick Gregory, "that's what I dug him for." (Quoted in Peter Goldman, *The Death and Life of Malcolm X.*)

wondered whether he was for real or, like so many other ghetto preachers, just another smooth operator in a big fine car, hustling little old ladies. On the street, people recognizing him from the old days would shout, "*Red! . . .* My *man! . . .* Red, this *can't* be you." [35] The fact is that Malcolm owned more or less what he had come out of prison with: his wristwatch, the clothes on his back, his briefcase, and his glasses. He lived frugally—monastically—in a modest house in Elmhurst, Queens. Above basic living expenses, he was given only pocket money. The house, the car, and even the spending money belonged to the Nation, to be enjoyed at the Messenger's pleasure.

In the twelve years since his imprisonment, Malcolm had never touched a woman. Muslim sisters noticed how he never looked at them, how he was always warning the brothers to be careful. Apart from temple business, he avoided them. He had no time for them, anyway. His every waking hour—eighteen to twenty, on average—was committed to the cause, his every thought for the emerging Nation. Telling the white man about himself was, after all, a full-time job.

Perhaps in part because of his family history and later experience on the ruthlessly exploitative ghetto streets, Malcolm had been conditioned to think of women as by nature fragile, weak, untrustworthy at best or, at worst, as nothing but another commodity. This view seems to have been reinforced by Black Muslim dogma, which taught that men and women were of different natures. Men were strong and women weak. It was for the man to command, and the woman to obey. The role of women, though important, was secondary. The husband was protector and provider; the woman his obedient helpmate, homemaker, and mother of his children. A man must respect a woman, certainly. But there was no such thing as equality between them. So narrow was the Nation of Islam's focus on racism from without that it lacked perspective on sexism from within.

Malcolm had known many women in the past. One or two he had even respected. But there was only one he would ever love: Betty X. Tall and brown, she was born in Detroit and had studied education at Tuskegee. When they met, she was in New York studying to become a nurse. She was struck at once by his seriousness and intensity. Her parents, too, were favorably impressed. He seemed so clean-cut, so well-mannered, so knowledgeable. In the winter of 1958, with Elijah Muhammad's blessing, they were married in a simple ceremony before the justice of the peace. Not that marriage mellowed Malcolm: He named his child—a girl, as it turned out, the first of six—Attilah, after the Hun who raided the empire of Rome.

He was everywhere at once, Nation-building. Never home for more than half the week, he might be away for months at a time. He was traveling so much that his wife kept two prepacked suitcases in the house so that, at a moment's notice, he could grab one and go. Even when not traveling, he brought work home with him, toiling till all hours of the night. Wife, mother, and switchboard operator, Betty was as likely to talk to her husband over the phone as face-to-face. It took immense patience to put up with it, and more than once she left him.

The Nation's public relations had been hitherto confined to scattered columns by Malcolm or Muhammad in black newspapers such as the *Amsterdam News* or *Pittsburgh Courier*. While setting up the Los Angeles Temple, Malcolm was able to visit the *Los Angeles Herald Dispatch* and thus observe firsthand the workings of a newspaper. This gave him the idea of starting a Muslim newspaper in New York. Always a quick study, with a secondhand camera Malcolm mastered the rudiments of photography, assembling texts and photos for a column of happenings in and around the Nation. Thus the birth of *Muhammad Speaks*, the militant monthly dedicated to "justice for the Black Man." [36]

**Betty X in 1964 with four of the six girls she and Malcolm would eventually have.**

With a circulation of over half a million, it was by far the most widely read black publication of the time.

Alex Haley, an unknown journalist recently retired from twenty years of service in the Coast Guard, prepared profiles on the Nation of Islam, its goals and its membership, for *Reader's Digest.* In rapid succession, an article appropriately titled "Muhammad Speaks" appeared, together with "The Hate that Hate Produced," a five-part television program in the *Newsbeat* series that aired in July 1959. And C. Eric Lincoln wrote *Black Muslims in America,* one of the first in-depth exposés of Malcolm and the movement, a book justly praised for both its rigor and its clarity.

Subsequent articles appeared in *Time* and *Newsweek.* European scholars were intrigued. French Canadian separatists were inspired. Whereas white liberals were appalled by the Nation's outright contempt for their goodwill, white racist extremists were delighted: At last, the two poles could agree on something; since they could not live together, they must live apart. The Ku Klux Klan (KKK) even offered the Nation money and land.

Before 1959, the Nation had perhaps 30,000 followers. "The Hate that Hate Produced" alone doubled that membership. Since a majority of recruits were either convicts or ex-convicts, the Bureau of Prisons had long been monitoring the Black Muslims. Now the FBI began putting pressure on the media to suppress news about the movement in the hope that it would wither away. But censorship only fueled public interest. Under constant surveillance from without by the FBI and from within by informants, the Nation's leadership tended to be guarded in its statements. Anything they did not wish to discuss—from religion to politics to the weather—was ritually referred to the Honorable Elijah Muhammad. And Elijah Muhammad himself was, as usual, enigmatic: "Those who say don't know, and those who know don't say." [37] And because they were so vague, the FBI kept an even closer eye on them. Bitterly, Elijah Muhammad

A member of the Nation sells copies of the hugely successful newspaper *Muhammad Speaks*, which Malcolm X established in 1961.

complained that if the bureau would infiltrate the KKK with even a fraction of the agents it wasted on the Black Muslims, lynching would cease altogether.

Ultimately, Malcolm X would be in some way responsible for most of the Nation's growth and for the establishment of most of its temples. Now advisory minister for several fledgling temples in addition to being minister for Temple No. 7, he no sooner founded a mosque in one city than he was off to establish the next. One trip, however, was special. On his first visit to the Deep South, Malcolm traveled to Atlanta, Georgia, home base of a rising young minister whose eloquence and influence rivaled and would soon surpass his own: the Reverend Dr. Martin Luther King, Jr.

# SOUTHERN CROSS

During the sixties, there were two pitched camps in the civil rights movement: Malcolm X and Martin Luther King, Jr., the Nation of Islam and the Southern Christian Leadership Conference (SCLC), star-and-crescent and southern cross.

Malcolm was a representative product of the northern ghetto. The world into which he was born asked nothing of him and expected less. Martin's warm and loving household was a stark contrast to Malcolm's. On January 15, 1929, Martin Luther King, Jr., was born into the middle class in Atlanta, the so-called capital of the New South, a city with a historically substantial black middle class. Like Malcolm's, Martin's father was a minister and placed high expectations on his oldest son.

But even in the black mecca of Atlanta, the city "too busy to hate," there was racism. Schools, restaurants, theaters, and housing were segregated. There were "colored only" signs on drinking fountains, in waiting rooms and rest rooms. There were lynchings and Ku Klux Klan violence. Martin hated whites early on. It was only in the integrated atmosphere of the university that he overcame some of his racial prejudices. Much earlier than Malcolm, he saw that not all whites were evil or racist. These early experiences with discrimination left him not hostile but determined.

The Reverend Martin
Luther King, Jr.

Martin Luther King was still a boy when Malcolm was attending his first UNIA meetings. Like Malcolm, Martin despised the tendency of conservative, church-going blacks to await the good life in the hereafter. But he was a negotiator rather than a fighter. He believed in the way of the cross, the redeeming power of suffering. He saw religion as a way to improve the plight of black Americans in the here and now. Martin understood the crucial role of the church as a surrogate providing social, political, and cultural cohesion in the face of slavery's systematic breakdown of the black family. And, like Malcolm, he felt a sense of duty, of obligation to a cause, a higher calling. But unlike Malcolm, Martin was encouraged in his love of learning. By the age of fifteen, he was attending Morehouse College. By twenty-two, while Malcolm was still serving time in prison for robbery, Martin was already an ordained minister.

Malcolm and Martin shared an admiration for Mohandas (Mahatma) Gandhi, who started his career as an obscure lawyer in British-ruled South Africa and ultimately became the great Indian nationalist leader. Determined first to win the civil rights denied Indian immigrants in South Africa and later the independence of the Indian subcontinent itself from British colonial rule, Gandhi had "twisted a knot in the British Lion's tail," [38] as Malcolm put it. In divinity school, King began to explore the writings of Gandhi.

Inspired by the teachings of Christ, the writings of Russian novelist Leo Tolstoy, and the example of Henry David Thoreau's *Civil Disobedience*, Gandhi advocated a strategy of passive resistance to British colonial rule. Confident that the justice of the Indian cause would prevail, he exhorted Indian civil servants to resign their posts and convinced the entire population to boycott British goods and institutions, and to refuse to pay taxes. Squatters blocked the streets, refusing to move and enduring brutal beatings at the hands of police. In and out of

MALCOLM X

**ON MARTIN LUTHER KING, JR.**

**He got the peace prize, and we got the problem.**

Interview with
Claude Lewis,
December 1964

jail, Gandhi himself dressed in the loincloth and shawl of the untouchable caste to protest India's antiquated system of hereditary inequality and went on countless hunger strikes. Revered as a saint, Mahatma Gandhi advocated Christian and Muslim ethics as well as Hindu. He was assassinated in 1948 by a Hindu protesting Gandhi's tolerance toward Muslims.

Under Gandhi's influence, Martin Luther King began to explore the power of "soul force" to counter social hatred. Martin later traveled in India, where he was inspired by the Indian boycott of British goods. Gandhi's nonviolent protest, Martin believed, could be applied to the struggle for civil rights in the South.

The term "civil rights" is most frequently associated with the struggle of African Americans against racism, but it likewise pertains to the struggle of any oppressed minority against religious persecution, sexism, or prejudice directed at a physical handicap or sexual orientation. Encompassing economic and social as well as racial domains, civil rights are most broadly defined as guarantees of free speech, press, and religion, as well as equal protection under the law.

Slavery was only a brutal extreme of discrimination. With the arrival of enslaved Africans in Jamestown, Virginia, in 1619, the black civil rights movement was born. The struggle for freedom, justice, and equality in North America has been not the story of a single war but of recurring battles.

In the South, the fifties were years of crucial transformation in black leadership. Previously, litigation and good-faith advocacy had been the principal agents of change in civil rights. The leadership was more aggressive in its demands now and more varied in its tactics. In 1954, King became pastor of the Dexter Avenue Baptist Church in Montgomery, Alabama. On May 17 of that same year, the Supreme Court in *Brown* v. *Topeka*

**Mohandas Gandhi**

declared segregation in public schools unconstitutional and ordered their desegregation "with all deliberate speed."

At the end of 1955, the young pastor at the Dexter Avenue Church took the civil rights movement in a new direction. In December, housekeeper and seamstress Rosa Parks was arrested for refusing to give up her bus seat to a white man. Encouraged by *Brown* v. *Topeka*, Martin Luther King organized a black boycott of the bus system that lasted throughout 1956. The Supreme Court ruled in December of that year that bus segregation was unconstitutional. The Montgomery Bus Boycott marked a more militant tack. The civil rights movement was becoming more confrontational—and more effective.

National publicity on the bus boycott catapulted King to the forefront. In 1957, joined by his closest associate Ralph David Abernathy, Andrew Young, later congressman from Georgia and ambassador to the United Nations, and other black clergymen of the South, King formed the SCLC, serving as its first president. Despite differences in philosophy on the part of the various civil rights groups and escalating violence on the part of reactionaries, the leadership generally agreed to follow Martin Luther King's principle of nonviolent protest.

In 1957, encouraged by the Supreme Court's stance in *Brown* v. *Topeka*, nine black children in Little Rock, Arkansas, took the matter of school desegregation into their own hands. With the assistance of Daisy Bates, Arkansas president of the NAACP, they attended an all-white high school in defiance of racist mobs and so forced President Dwight D. Eisenhower to send in federal troops to protect them.

Martin Luther King moved to Atlanta in 1960, thus strategically positioning himself to spearhead the civil rights movement. The year before he had been in India, and he returned more convinced than ever that nonviolent resistance was the most effective means to attain civil rights. By this time, it had spread to the colleges, where the Student Nonviolent Coordinating

Committee (SNCC), with King's blessing, conducted sit-ins and voter registration drives and rural literacy programs. In 1961, groups of idealistic young people participated in the CORE Freedom Rides, busload caravans of protesters desegregating interstate buses and terminals in the Deep South. These, too, met with violent resistance from southern whites, who firebombed one of the buses. A week later, Attorney General Robert F. Kennedy was forced to send federal troops to Montgomery, Alabama, to keep the peace.

In 1963, King led a march in Birmingham, Alabama, followed by voter registration drives and protests for better housing and education. Racist violence continued to escalate in spite of King's commitment to nonviolent tactics. The year culminated with a massive general protest on August 28 in the March on Washington, a call for congressional action on civil rights.

But the various civil rights groups were ill coordinated. And none was under heavier attack from within the movement than the Nation of Islam. The NAACP, which was opposed to racial extremism, saw the Nation as just another extremist group. As far as the Nation was concerned, the Urban League was a black front for a white agenda. As the Muslims gained strength, other black leaders worried. The atmosphere of interracial cooperation built up painstakingly over generations was being threatened by the new militancy. The Muslims were accused of preaching a doctrine of hatred and black supremacy no better than the white supremacy they challenged, thereby jeopardizing what little goodwill there was between blacks and whites.

At best, the other leaders saw the Black Muslims as a useful, if not entirely creditable, movement whose proposed solution to the American dilemma was simply not viable. Some blacks secretly admired its ends, if not its means. Elijah Muhammad might be an embarrassing fanatic and a charlatan, perverting Orthodox Islamic doctrine, but he was partly right. And anybody who could get blacks to quit crime, save money, and eat better

**ON CHRISTIANITY**

I find it difficult [to believe] that . . . Christians accuse [Black Muslims] of teaching racial supremacy or . . . hatred, because their own history and . . . teachings are filled with it.

Interview with
William Kunstler,
March 1960

Right: In 1961, a bus filled with Freedom Riders was set on fire by whites in Anniston, Alabama. Passengers were attacked as they fled to escape the flames.
Below: The 1963 March on Washington, a massive gathering in support of civil rights led by King (center). Malcolm dismissed the peaceful, integrated march as "the farce on Washington."

did more for the community than all the welfare agencies put together.

Early on, King dismissed the Nation as a fanatical hate group. Malcolm, for his part, publicly despised what he called the "Bishop Chickenwings" [39] of the black ministry and all the other conservatives he saw as soft on the white man. The NAACP and Urban League were class movements; the Nation was a mass movement with a goal of five million members by 1965. Thurgood Marshall, not known for tact or discretion, called the Muslims "a bunch of thugs organized from prisons and jails and financed, I am sure, by some Arab Group." [40] Malcolm in turn called Thurgood Marshall a "20th century Uncle Tom." [41]

King's efforts culminated in his receiving the Nobel Peace Prize, and in the passage of the Civil Rights Act of 1964. By the end of 1965, the shocking violence of Bloody Sunday in Montgomery, Alabama, had been seared into the American consciouness. The Voting Rights Act had been signed. Civil rights for blacks were now protected under the law.

Social realities were another matter, though. The CORE Freedom Riders who had come gallantly down South faced problems of their own up North.

**Malcolm X during a
speech in Harlem.**

In 1963, Malcolm X was still a fringe figure in the struggle for civil rights, at least as far as the media was concerned. Two things soon changed that forever.

First, there was Elijah Muhammad. The long speeches and huge rallies took their toll on the Messenger's already failing health. At the Nation's expense, he moved into a newly acquired estate in Phoenix, Arizona. "Brother Malcolm," he said, "I want you to become well known. Because if you are well known, it will make *me* better known." The Messenger warned him, however: "You will grow to be hated. People get jealous of public figures." [42] This pushed Malcolm toward center stage. Mysteriously, his unlisted number had gotten out, and from that day forward, no sooner did he put the receiver down than the phone rang again—at home, at Muslim restaurants, in airports.

Speaking engagements poured in from everywhere. Malcolm appeared face-to-face with academics before television audiences numbering in the millions. Practicing every spare moment, he became a master of the media, dazzling audiences with his rapid-fire delivery. In verbal combat he was relentless, attacking opponents with a barrage of facts, figures, and acid wit. Malcolm learned to work up the audience, relying on shock tactics to an extent that ultimately proved his undoing. He never allowed himself to get emotional or lose his cool, but did, however, pander shamelessly to the deepest hopes or fears of a given audience. He was called the angriest black man in America. And perhaps he was. The voice of Islam, the "Messenger's messenger," [43] Minister Malcolm X came to be regarded as one of the most visible and articulate spokesmen in the struggle for civil rights.

Then there was Alex Haley, who had already interviewed Malcolm for *Playboy*. Later that year, Haley sat waiting in the restaurant of Temple No. 7 for what would prove an even more important interview.

Tall, handsome, and confident to the point of cockiness, Malcolm seemed to fill the room as he entered. Haley noted his spartan style: the sober suit, spit-shined shoes, leather briefcase, severe spectacles, and serious expression that made him resemble the attorney he had always dreamed of being. He walked briskly. There was a sense of urgency about everything he said and did. Always anxious to see who came and went, he insisted on the seat facing the door.

Malcolm was fidgety. This was hardly surprising, since he seemed to live on coffee and cream—the only thing, he quipped, that he liked integrated. He looked distractedly, obsessively, at his watch. Rigorously punctual, he kept appointments with journalists, ministers, and heads of state seemingly around the clock. His schedule was inhuman. As often as four times weekly, he crossed and recrossed the country, sleeping mostly on planes and in airports and keeping fanatically to a grueling timetable of television, radio, and public appearances—sometimes all on the same day.

He had become a celebrity, known on sight to highway motorists and frequent fliers who, presumably on their way to the rest room, would one by one file slowly past to nod, to speak, or just to stare. People even asked for autographs. Martin Luther

King was curious to hear what he was like. He was the most electric personality Haley had ever encountered. But there seemed to be more than one Malcolm X. In public, he was smoldering intensity: controlled, calculated, menacing. In private, though his manner was direct, he could be gentle, courteous, even charming. He had wit and humor; he might smile, he might laugh. Even so, he was always dead serious.

Haley had an idea. Why not portray this other Malcolm X, the man behind the racist stereotype, the proud man, the sensitive man, the highly intelligent man? Intrigued, Malcolm let himself be talked into telling the story of his life—not, he was convinced, out of vanity or personal glory but to set the record straight, to give living testimony to the Messenger's power to do miracles among men. Dead or alive, Malcolm knew he would be used as a symbol. He also knew he had only so long to fulfill his life's work, and death could come at any time. The thing was to be armed with his own version of the truth, a last will and testament, the story not only of his life but of all the lives of those whose dreams were yet deferred, of those in whom there still festered a rage as violent, if not as articulate, as his own. Besides, given his hectic pace, this might be the only chance to stop, to think, to put things in perspective.

Then and there, *The Autobiography of Malcolm X* was born. For two years, they worked on the book. Maintaining a delicate balance between artistic integrity, historical truth, and the subject's own version of the story, Haley brought Malcolm's life alive, crafting a narrative of artfully enduring simplicity. Through Haley, millions of readers—many of them white— gained insight into the man. The Nation's spokesman began to eclipse the organization he sought to represent. To most whites and to many segments of the black community, Black Muslim doctrine remained largely unpalatable, whereas Malcolm became a subject of controversy—a star.

The very term "Nation of Islam" implies both social, political, and economic black nationalism and Islamic religion. The movement advocated economic self-sufficiency and cooperation among blacks as well as a strict, if unorthodox, Islamic code in matters of diet, dress, morality, and prayer. Though it remains the largest and best-known black nationalist organization, the Nation of Islam was only one of many groups active in the civil rights era of the 1950s and 1960s, and by no means the most extreme.

Essentially, black nationalism was a reaction to white racism. Just as nations define themselves in opposition to their neighbors, so blacks shut out from white society espoused not only black pride but, at its most extreme, a rejection of all things white. At best, the Nation of Islam's philosophy was an earnest, if misguided, attempt to lift the despised African American up from the trash heap of white society to "the same level with all other civilized and independent nations and peoples."[44] At worst, much of the Nation's rhetoric amounted to little more than racist hatemongering indistinguishable from that which it condemned. Malcolm X, as one writer put it, did not so much "teach" hatred as preach to the hatred that many black people already knew.

Elijah Muhammad admired Marcus Garvey; his black nationalism was to the 1950s and early 1960s what Garveyism had been to the 1920s. Convinced that freedom without capital was only another kind of slavery, Elijah Muhammad preached that America's 22 million so-called Negroes were a nation within a nation, yearning to breathe free. Rather than appealing to the conscience of whites, as other civil rights groups did, Muhammad sought a completely separate and independent economy. The collective income of African Americans, he pointed out, exceeded that of many European nations. Yet in the ghetto, white shopkeepers fled at sundown, took their money back to suburbs where blacks were not allowed to live, and asserted control by means of a hostile police force tantamount to an occupying army.

Several times weekly, Black Muslims attended meetings where they were exhorted to hold steady jobs, live within their means, donate a percentage of their earnings toward the Nation, and abstain from the drinking, drugging, and petty crime that kept blacks down and fed the purses of white profiteers. So long as whites controlled the economy, blacks were at their mercy. Muslims believed that welfare fostered laziness and dependency. Blacks should own their own homes, patronize their own businesses, hire their own people, and become self-sufficient, just like other ethnic groups. The only way they would gain the respect of whites or anybody else was through self-respect.

Despite these declarations of independence, the Nation demanded that the government turn over at least one and as many as ten states as reparations, since blacks had worked, Malcolm said, "300 years without a payday." [45] If the United States could finance Israel and even hostile nations all over the world, why couldn't it finance a black nation here at home?

The peak years for the Nation of Islam were from 1959 to 1964. Under Wallace Fard, the Black Muslims had been a mere cult, numbering perhaps eight thousand. Under Elijah Muhammad, the cult became a movement. And under Malcolm X, that movement became a force. From a few faithful huddling in ghetto storefronts, it had grown into an organization of truly national proportions, with hundreds of thousands of followers, accredited schools, health clinics, radio stations, coast-to-coast real estate, a fleet of planes, and even its own highly trained and disciplined army, the Fruit of Islam—guardians, so to speak, of the faith.

As the Nation was one movement among many, so was Malcolm's one of many black voices in the swelling chorus of the civil rights movement. "His speeches," argues Professor Henry Louis Gates, "are masterpieces of the rhetorical arts.

**ON SEGREGATION**

Segregation is that which is forced upon inferiors by superiors. Separation is done voluntarily by two equals. . . . The Negro schools in the Negro community are controlled by whites, . . . the economy of the Negro community is controlled by whites. And since the Negro . . . community is controlled or regulated by outsiders, it is a segregated community. . . . Muslims who follow the Honorable Elijah Muhammad are as much against segregation as we are against integration. We are against segregation because it is unjust and we are against integration because [it is] a false solution to a real problem.

WUST interview,
May 1963

65 ★ )

**Escorted by the Fruit of Islam, Malcolm walks to a Harlem rally at 115th Street and Lenox Avenue in 1963; three to four thousand people came to hear him speak.**

More than Martin Luther King, Jr., more than any of the black nationalists, Malcolm X was a *writer*."

In truth, though, except for collections of scattered statements and his collaboration with Alex Haley, Malcolm "wrote" nothing. He was a master of radio and television—media more suited to catchy sound bytes than to rigorous argument. In the reckless immediacy of the live, on-air moment, the footage and broadcasts are fascinating to watch. In the stillness of quiet reflection, the published speeches often don't hold up. Many have not even survived. Much of Malcolm's rhetoric was less conclusive rebuttal than mere one-upmanship. His learning was wide, not deep, as his misstatements of fact tend to show. Malcolm X was less a thinker than an activist, less a writer than a rapper.

Though Malcolm grew rapidly through his exposure to the wider world of ideas, in some ways he remained intellectually immature. He once went so far as to say that the murder of six million Jews during the Holocaust had been their own fault, that they had "brought it on themselves." [46] Naturally, this drew charges of anti-Semitism. The Nation defended itself by arguing that, since Black Muslims identified themselves with Arabs, and since Jews, like Arabs, are Semites, its statements were not anti-Semitic, only anti-Zionist.

Nor was the otherwise austere Minister Malcolm X above vanity. News broadcasts were the only television he permitted himself, but these he viewed with relish, as fascinated by his own media image as was the world at large, and obviously enjoying the performance.

In the beginning, most middle-class blacks were hostile, suspicious, or contemptuous of the Nation of Islam. There was also envy among rival civil rights organizations, which were anxious about the attention given Black Muslims by a press that seemed always eager to exaggerate the worst aspects of black America. Malcolm felt the NAACP was a paper tiger that could

**ON TRUTH**

**I'm telling it like it is!**

*The Autobiography of Malcolm X*

change laws but not enforce them. Conservatives criticized the SCLC for pushing reform too fast; the Nation criticized it for not pushing fast enough. Attacks in the press became vicious and more frequent, with liberals turning on Malcolm even faster than racists had. (Outright bigots he respected; they, at least, were honest.) White leaders accused him of extremism, black leaders of polarizing the community, and conservative intellectuals of being just plain wrong. They threw up their hands in collective exasperation. Couldn't he *see* that integration was the answer to the "Negro Problem"? Wasn't separatism exactly what white racists had wanted since Reconstruction? If he was a demagogue, Malcolm shrugged, so what? The root of the word, he explained, citing Socrates and Jesus as perhaps the greatest of "demagogues," [47] was Greek for "leader of the people."

Black Muslims shared the KKK's hatred of integration. Whites, they argued, were "directly responsible for not only the *presence* of this black man in America, but also for the *condition* in which we find this black man here." [48] White society was corrupt, its downfall inevitable. It hardly behooved blacks to integrate into it. Their only hope was to secede, establish their own homeland, and demand complete and total separation. Separation meant black control, black pride. A separate nation, a separate peace, that was the blacks' only hope of achieving their own culture, identity, and self-respect.

The attitude of conservative black leaders was that African Americans were just that: Americans. Their problems were America's problems—and vice versa. Integration was, to conservative blacks, not synonymous with assimilation. Far from mere lunch counter privileges integration meant, as in any organism—social or mechanical—the inseparable functioning of a unit, which would benefit if properly aligned and if not would wreck the whole.

Malcolm X was contemptuous of the "turn-the-other-cheek revolution" of civil rights leaders whose ostensible goal was "coffee with a cracker." As far as he was concerned, German Jews had been history's darkest example of a people fatally deluded by integration. Recognized among Germany's greatest writers, artists, and composers, they had won half its Nobel prizes and published its most influential newspapers. Cutting themselves off from their roots, some had even intermarried with non-Jews, changing their religion, names, and even noses—none of which had spared them Hitler's hell.

Whites were alarmed by the Nation of Islam. Did the fact that the Fruit of Islam was being trained in the use of firearms and hand-to-hand combat mean the Nation was planning an all-out race war? Black Muslims were taught to do unto others as they would have others do unto them, but not to turn the other cheek when attacked. While Malcolm never openly advocated violence, the belligerent image he projected seemed to threaten as much. He argued that nonviolence was for little old ladies in the backs of Alabama buses, not black men. All that suffering, and for what? If the law failed to protect blacks from white attack, said Malcolm, blacks should defend themselves—with arms, if necessary.

A product of the North, Malcolm had never seen the South before his trip to Atlanta. Though they later become respected rivals, at one point Malcolm's contempt for Martin was such that, in private, he swore that when he finally met Martin he would bust him in the jaw—just to see how "nonviolent" he really was. For his part, Martin accused Malcolm of rabble-rousing, saying he did blacks a disservice by criticizing without offering any practical alternative. Likewise, within the wider black community, the main criticism of the Black Muslims was that they "*talk* tough, but they never *do* anything." [49] "I'm not a politician," said Malcolm. "I'm not a Democrat, I'm not a Republican, and I don't even consider myself an American." [50] As a rule, Black Muslims didn't participate in electoral politics. Remaining largely aloof, they threatened to exercise power at

**ON NONVIOLENCE**
Our religion teaches us to be intelligent. Be peaceful, be courteous, obey the law, respect everyone; but if someone lays a hand on you, send him to the cemetery.

WUST interview, May 1963

**ON EXTREMISM**

Yes, I'm an extremist.
The black race . . . is in
extremely bad condition.

*The Autobiography
of Malcolm X*

the polls, but chose not to. After all, they could be counted if they registered. On this much, Malcolm and Martin agreed: "A Negro in Mississippi cannot vote," said King, "and a Negro in New York believes [he or she] has nothing for which to vote." [51]

It's instructive to compare the public-speaking styles of the two leaders. For the most part, Malcolm's strategy of combating racism was to fight fire with rhetorical fire. Where Malcolm's attitude was an Old Testament "eye for an eye," Martin's was a New Testament "turn the other cheek." By far more influential among the black middle class, Martin's characteristic venue was the pulpit. As minister of Temple No. 7 in New York, Malcolm headed the single most powerful of the Nation's mosques. His pulpit was all Harlem, where for hours at a time he mesmerized crowds of thousands. Speaking extemporaneously was something that came more naturally to the street-wise orator than it did to the formally educated seminarian.

Martin Luther King's transcendent moment came in August 1963 at the March on Washington, coordinated by the leaders of the five major civil rights organizations and attended by a quarter million people from all over the nation—nearly half of them white. Malcolm would characterize this peaceful gathering, before which Martin delivered his classic "I Have a Dream" speech, as the "farce on Washington." [52]

But differences between them should not obscure their similarities. Born just four years apart, both became ministers, and both were assassinated at the age of thirty-nine. What they also had in common was the fact that, due to the "extreme political limitations" [53] placed on black men, they preached because they could do little else: politics was out; business was out; government service was out. But as preachers, they could be politicians, businessmen, and public servants all at once. Malcolm, who might have been a lawyer, became a preacher by default.

King remains the patron saint of the civil rights movement; Malcolm has not received as much attention. Toward the end,

A crowd hangs on the words of the speaker— Malcolm X.

**ON REVOLUTION**

People involved in a revolution don't become part of the system; they destroy the system . . . . The Negro revolution is no revolution because it condemns the system and then asks the system it has condemned to accept them . . . .

Interview with A. B. Spellman, May 1964

however, King became more militant, and Malcolm more conciliatory. King began to urge, if not black power, then at least black pride; if not black nationalism, then at least black economic well-being. Having learned through hard experience the limits of civil disobedience and passive resistance, King even began to explore the possibility of "temporary segregation." Toward the end, their paths converged. As one writer argues: "They complemented and corrected each other." [54]

Malcolm came to grudgingly acknowledge the role of Dr. King and other southern leaders in the struggle for civil rights, saying, "Black people have advanced further when they have seen they had to rise up against a system that they clearly saw was outright against them. Under the . . . liberals, the Northern Negro became a beggar. But the Southern Negro, facing the . . . snarling white man, rose up to battle . . . for his freedom, long before it happened in the North." [55]

King was much less successful in the North, where the issue was not voting rights but jobs, which could not be created by sit-ins. He was met with resentment from black Baptists in Chicago, the Nation of Islam headquarters, and by the armed resistance of neo-Nazis and the KKK. And nonviolence was not attractive to people in urban ghettos who had long suffered from police brutality. They did respond, however, to the idea of black empowerment.

Originally perceived as conservative, Martin has come to seem far more revolutionary than Malcolm imagined. "Even in the 'nonviolent' expression posited by Martin Luther King, there was an activist aspect that made Elijah Muhammad's 'noninvolvement' in politics seem openly conservative." [56] Martin's actions, however tame, were more effective than Malcolm's talk, however militant. Martin willingly broke the law if the law was unjust—or tried to change it. His dream, that one day men would be judged not by the color of their skin but by the content of their character, was more radical than the country was prepared for.

Malcolm was committed to uplifting the black race. Martin's vision was perhaps even more audacious: uplifting the *human* race, challenging America to live up to "the true meaning of its creed" that all men are created equal. He was a visionary who believed in America more than America believed in herself.

Malcolm, on the other hand, despite—or perhaps because of—his hybrid nature, lacked appreciation for what is truly unique about the music of the North American soul: the extent to which it is both unmistakably black and unmistakably American, something to be comprehended rather than condemned. Malcolm seemed not to appreciate how profoundly American he really was. Ironically, for one who accused whites of being "tone deaf to the total orchestration of humanity,"[57] Malcolm seemed a little unmusical at times.

**Malcolm talks with a group of college students. By 1964, he was a frequent speaker on campus.**

## THE ENLIGHTENMENT

"Friends and enemies . . . ." [58] Addressing the Law School Forum, Malcolm glanced out the window and suddenly realized he was looking at his Boston burglary ring's old hideout. Once again, he thanked Allah that the Messenger had rescued him from the penitentiary, the madhouse, or the morgue. For here he was, a new man, at Harvard.

The more Malcolm spoke on behalf of Elijah Muhammad, the greater the response. Letters poured in from everywhere, most of them from whites, and surprisingly few of them death threats. Thanks in part to *Black Muslims in America,* then required reading in colleges and universities, and to the television program "The Hate that Hate Produced," he had now addressed audiences at over fifty famous colleges and universities, including Brown, Columbia, Harvard, and Yale. *Playboy* magazine, hugely popular on campus, carried a candid interview in May 1963. *Life, Newsweek*, and "Meet the Press" requested cover stories or guest appearances. By 1964, Malcolm X was among the most sought-after speakers on the lecture circuit, second only to presidential candidate Barry Goldwater.

Malcolm liked college audiences best. They were among the most open-minded anywhere. They seemed . . . more intense, more intelligent. For hours at a time, he spoke and fielded questions from the best and brightest young minds in the country. Or he sat in on panel discussions with scholars in sociology, philosophy, history, or religion. He found it exhilarating to compete in the field of learning and ideas. Reminding him of his long hours reading and debating in prison, these public speaking engagements were an education in themselves. This exposure brought Malcolm into contact with whites who were not devils, who stimulated him, nourished him. One student on whom Malcolm X made a lasting impression, and who would herself become famous as an activist, was Brandeis undergraduate Angela Davis. The students, it seemed, were America's only hope.

They also made him reconsider his racial hard line. Most agreed with the Nation's view of the problem, if not with its proposed solution. In particular, the bit about the "blue-eyed devil" always seemed to put them off. Malcolm was quick to qualify: "We are not speaking of any *individual* white man. We are speaking of the collective white man's *historical* record. We are speaking of the collective white man's cruelties, and evils, and greed, that have seen him *act* like a devil toward the non-white man." [59]

For some reason, Elijah Muhammad disapproved of these college speaking engagements. Was he, because of his own lack of education, jealous of Malcolm's gifts? Or was he afraid of what might result from them? For it was during Malcolm's exposure to this wider world of ideas that he got his first glimpses into what Muslim students from the Middle East and North Africa tactfully hinted was "true Islam." [60] He came in contact with eminent Islamic scholars, one of whom said, "No man has believed perfectly until he wishes for his brother what he wishes for himself" as he handed Malcolm a letter authorizing him to make a pilgrimage to Mecca. [61]

As supreme leader of the Nation of Islam, Elijah Muhammad insisted on submission. More than once, he reminded Malcolm that in "any organization, someone must be the boss." [62] One of their policy disputes proved fateful. Malcolm had restrained himself when white racists murdered NAACP field secretary Medgar Evers in Mississippi. He had even held back when they bombed a church in Birmingham, Alabama, killing four innocent young girls. But when President John F. Kennedy was assassinated at Dallas, Texas, on November 22, 1963, Malcolm could restrain himself no longer. It seemed to him that this was God's judgment, the inevitable outcome of America's climate of duplicity, hatred, and violence. Those who lived by the sword must die by the sword, and this tragedy, though it had grieved the nation and the world, was only, he shrugged, "a case of the chickens coming home to roost."

Elijah Muhammad himself had been scheduled to speak that day, but canceled out of respect, instructing the Nation's leadership likewise to refrain from comment. The day after Malcolm's remark, Muhammad silenced him, forbidding him to make public statements for ninety days. Only a few months before, Malcolm had been appointed national minister. During a Philadelphia rally that would prove their last public appearance together, Muhammad had publicly embraced Malcolm before the audience, proclaiming him his most faithful and industrious minister. But something was now afoot. Malcolm, it seemed, could remain Muhammad's mascot provided he toed the party line. Once he stepped across, he was silenced. The silent treatment, he knew, was the beginning of the end for him as one of Muhammad's ministers. "I hadn't hustled in the streets for years for nothing. I knew when I was being set up." [63]

The petty jealousy the Messenger had warned him of proved prophetic. Voices whispered in Elijah Muhammad's ear. Always on television and in the newspapers, flying coast-to-coast, Malcolm, some said, was taking all the credit for the Nation's rise. And the sheer size of the crowds he drew was alarming, to the Black Muslim hierarchy as well as to other watchful eyes. The

**ON HOLY WAR**

The war of Armageddon has already started. . . . God is using nature as one of his many weapons. He is sending hurricanes so fast that [the blue-eyed devils] can't name them. He is drowning them in floods and causing their cars to crash and their airplanes cannot stay up in the sky. Their boats are sinking because Allah controls all things and he is using all methods to begin to wipe the devils off the planet, [and] the enemy is dying of diseases that have never been so deadly.

**The FBI Files**

halls were always jammed: seven thousand at a rally in Harlem; eight thousand at the University of California. Malcolm was becoming too powerful. Malcolm was trying to take over. Malcolm must be stopped. Muhammad knew that Malcolm could potentially split the membership, taking the vital New York constituency with him. Muhammad vividly remembered the battle for succession within the movement thirty years before, when Fard had disappeared. It must not be allowed to happen again. Nobody—not even Malcolm X—could be allowed to stand in the way. He soon became convinced that Malcolm was plotting war against him. The Messenger feared for his life, and the Messenger must be protected at all costs.

Beyond these territorial jealousies, there was the very real struggle for financial control of the burgeoning Black Muslim empire. There were the lucrative businesses, the tens of millions of dollars in assets, the private jet. Not even Elijah Muhammad could live forever. And when he died, who would take control? Would there be a purge? And, if so, who would be in and who left out? Malcolm "was [caught] in a power struggle," as one writer put it, "and there was no way he could have survived it without having equal competing power, and he didn't have it." [64]

The worst thing about the gag rule was the inactivity, the sitting at home with nothing to do and nowhere to go. "I was a zombie then—like all Muslims—I was hypnotized, pointed in a certain direction and told to march." [65] Elijah Muhammad could silence him, but he could no longer persuade him. A man should think for himself—no matter what his position.

Then something happened that further shook Malcolm's faith. As early as 1955, he had heard but refused to heed the rumors. He could not—would not—believe the Messenger was capable of the things they said about him: Elijah Muhammad had had sex with several young Muslim secretaries. Some of them, it was said, had even had his "divine babies". [66] The Black Muslims saw themselves as pillars of virtue, thus proving themselves, in their own minds, morally invulnerable to the society that despised them. Any lapse on the part of Elijah Muhammad might prove his puritanical evangelism to be a righteous fraud, and now he was exposed to his most trusting disciple as the ultimate hypocrite.

"I felt as though something in *nature* had failed, like the sun, or the stars." [67] Loyal to a fault, Malcolm had exalted the Messenger as a living symbol of moral and spiritual perfection. He had imagined him without weaknesses, without failings, irreproachable, infallible—a prophet, like Jesus, like Buddha—with the power to change history by changing men's minds. "I had actually believed that if Mr. Muhammad was not God, then he surely stood next."[68] Malcolm offered up his own life as testimonial to the transforming power of his message. "He had virtually raised me from the dead." [69]

Elijah Muhammad was human, not the god Malcolm needed him to be. And, being human, he could not live up to Malcolm's unrealistic expectations. "I was his most faithful servant, and I know today that I did believe in him more firmly than he believed in himself." [70] In the year to come, Malcolm would undergo a psychological and spiritual crisis. What was worse, Malcolm had been made to look like a fool—a sucker. The hustler had himself been hustled. In his will to believe, it never occurred to Malcolm that he had been from the beginning exploited like some needy adolescent in the stable of a practiced pimp. A supreme hustler, Elijah Muhammad used much the same means, albeit with a different angle and to a different end.

Now convinced that he would never be reinstated, Malcolm officially broke with Elijah Muhammad and the Nation of Islam in early March 1964. He still hoped to maintain good relations with Elijah Muhammad. Accordingly, he declined to discuss their differences in public, saying only that they had agreed to disagree. Then Muhammad himself began to attack. Malcolm retaliated. He persuaded the two former secretaries to swear out affidavits that they had carried on affairs with Muhammad, accusing him of fathering their four children, and to file paternity suits against him. He also began making veiled accusations of religious fraud on Elijah Muhammad's part.

Malcolm was even more devastated to discover that Elijah Muhammad had not only failed but betrayed him. The rumors and veiled threats had begun spreading as early as 1961. Now an FBI wiretap revealed an unidentified man saying, "Just tell him he's as good as dead." [71] Not long afterward, the first reward for his assassination—ten thousand dollars, allegedly from the white Louisiana Citizens Council—came over the wire. Malcolm suspected that there were others plotting his downfall. When he heard that the assassination order had been issued by none other than Elijah Muhammad, he was shocked. From that moment on, he knew he would be murdered. He just never knew when. "I could conceive death," he said. "I could not conceive betrayal." [72] He had less than one year to live.

Malcolm was a man at the crossroads. The break with Elijah Muhammad was a bitter emotional blow. The numbers were clear. When he had joined the Nation of Islam in 1952, its membership totaled perhaps four thousand. Malcolm had been instrumental in establishing the powerful New York City temples in addition to the more than one hundred mosques in fifty states. By 1963—due largely to his own tireless efforts—the membership had peaked at about 400,000, making Elijah Muhammad one of the most influential black men in America. He reviewed the twelve years he had spent in the service of Elijah Muhammad. The Messenger had reached out to him in prison, in the darkness where he lay. But envy had driven a wedge between them. He had identified so completely with the movement that he could not imagine life, could not imagine self, without it. He had become synonymous with the Nation of Islam. And the Nation, much to the resentment of some, had become largely synonymous with him. What had been a powerfully vital movement had hardened into a bureaucracy of self-serving theocrats. Once again, Malcolm felt like a fatherless child.

Malcolm began to find the thinking of most black leaders limited and unimaginative. If only they would begin to think internationally! He had wanted the Nation to go international, but Elijah Muhammad had not. The Nation, he felt, had reached a dead end anyway, fatally alienating itself from the principal outlets for black rage—sports and entertainment. Its focus was too narrow, its morality too restrictive. African Americans, he felt, should start to think of themselves less as a minority and more as one of the world's nonwhite majorities, a political and religious force to be reckoned with throughout the Middle East, Africa, Asia, Europe, and South America. The Americas alone constituted a total black population of 80 million.

Where should he go? What should he do? First, he must face facts. He had no money, but he had something almost as valuable: notoriety. He was news, and he was headquartered in New York City, the news capital. What was more, he had range. He could speak at Harvard or in Harlem. He commanded the attention and respect of the grass roots, with which the other so-called Negro leaders were hopelessly out of touch. In New York, at least, there were also many non-Muslims who might be willing to follow where he led. Hadn't the media said that he was the only black man in America who "could stop a race riot—or start one"? [73]

He dreamed of an organization that would help cure blacks of their spiritual, political, and economic ills. Unlike the Nation of Islam, such an organization would embrace all faiths. It would practice what the Muslims only preached. Such an organization would foster solidarity, instilling in the black community the dignity, pride, incentive, and confidence to "get up off its knees and back on its feet." [74]

On March 12, he founded the Muslim Mosque, Inc. (MMI), a black nationalist organization intended to provide religious, cultural, and moral leadership for the black community. The MMI, temporarily headquartered in Harlem's Hotel Theresa, ultimately evolved into the Organization of Afro-American Unity (OAAU), a nonreligious group established for the purpose of doing "whatever is necessary to bring the Negro struggle from the level of civil rights to the level of human rights." [75]

Conservative elements within the Nation were discontent with the lack of orthodoxy among the Black Muslims. Elijah Muhammad's own son Wallace eventually broke with him. After his father's death in 1975, Wallace broke away from Louis Farrakhan's more radical faction, downplaying militant nationalism, stressing patriotism, allowing whites to join, and seeking greater orthodoxy and unity with the Muslim world at large. Day by day, more and more disillusioned Muslims broke with the Nation and pledged allegiance to the OAAU. More and more non-Muslims followed suit. Liberal whites and others offered contributions and moral support. Some feminists believe that, while the Black Muslims thought women's liberation much less important than black male liberation, Malcolm became progressively more sympathetic to their cause after leaving the Nation of Islam.

Malcolm was now prepared to cooperate with civil rights leaders North and South. On March 26, 1964, he met with Martin Luther King, Jr., during a news conference at the Capitol. His subsequent public statements about King were considerably less hostile in tone. However divergent their means, the two were working, he said, toward similar ends.

The hajj, or pilgrimage to Mecca, is a religious observance symbolizing the attainment of physical and spiritual sanctity. Devout Muslims are required to make this pilgrimage at least once in their lifetime, if economically possible. En route to Mecca, Malcolm flew first to Cairo, Egypt. There were people from every corner of the globe—Africa, Asia, Europe—some

**Martin and Malcolm, during their first and only meeting in Washington, D.C., March 1964.**

still in their national costumes. It was like something out of *National Geographic.* "Throngs of people, obviously Muslims from everywhere, bound on the pilgrimage, were hugging and embracing," he recalled. "They were of all complexions, the whole atmosphere was of warmth and friendliness. The effect was as though I had just stepped out of a prison." [76]

Orthodox Islam celebrates the brotherhood of man, without regard to race or color. But of all that he experienced at Mecca, it was the feeling of brotherhood that inspired Malcolm most. Wherever he turned, people offered help and kindness. On the plane to Jeddah, he marveled, were "white, black, brown, red and yellow people, blue eyes and blond hair, and my kinky red hair—all together, all brothers! All honoring the same God Allah, all in turn giving equal honor to each other."[77] In what he later learned to have been the greatest hajj in history, he and his fellow Muslims had eaten from the same plate, drunk from the same cup, slept on the same rug, snored in the same sleep, and prayed to the same God—regardless of race, color, or nationality.

At Mecca, Malcolm discovered that Elijah Muhammad had corrupted the teachings of Orthodox Islam. He came to understand that the mad black scientist Yacub was merely an unfortunate example of the demonology common to many organized religions, and that this and other deliberate misrepresentations of historical Islam were frowned upon in the Holy Land. He began to realize, too, just how ignorant of Islamic ritual he really was. Feeling foolish, Malcolm shed his clothes and draped himself with the two white sheets all pilgrims wear, one around the loins and the other around the neck and shoulders. On his big feet were a pair of sandals, his money in a money belt, his passport, letter of authorization, and other important documentation in what looked to be a woman's pocketbook. Like a child, he followed along with the prayers, self-consciously unaware of what he was doing or what it might mean. Then, barefoot, sandals in hand, Malcolm approached the Great Mosque, the

Malcolm X in Egypt en route to Mecca, where he made his final transformation to El-Hajj Malik El-Shabazz. "I totally reject Elijah Muhammad's racist philosophy, which he has labeled 'Islam' only to fool and misuse gullible people." (From a letter Malcolm wrote to *The New York Times* from Mecca.)

House of God. Numb with awe and emotion, he entered. From afar, he saw pilgrims by the thousands throng the *Ka'ba*, the huge black stone in the middle, circling slowly, ritually, seven times around, in a pattern that resembled one continuous wave, chanting *Takbir!* ("God is great!"), *Takbir!*

For the first time, Malcolm had a vision of the unity of God and man. Not since his awakening in prison had he had a revelation of such magnitude. That day in the Holy City of Mecca was "the first time I had ever stood before the Creator . . . and felt like a complete human being. That morning was when I first began to perceive that 'white man,' as commonly used, means complexion only secondarily; primarily it described attitudes and actions. . . . That morning was the start of a radical alteration in my whole outlook about 'white men.'" [78]

Was this pious naivete? Was this opportune PR? Everyone who knew him believed entirely in his transformation after Mecca. But the fact is that Malcolm's views of "the blue-eyed devil" had begun to change when he first traveled abroad in 1959, a full five years before Mecca. On that first trip to Africa and the Middle East, Malcolm had been warmly received and praised throughout the Muslim world for the good work the Nation of Islam was doing among African Americans. He needn't, perhaps, have traveled so far to learn that the problem was not so much the "white man" as the racist American social, political, and economic climate that produced him.

Since 1960, seventeen African states had achieved independence. The impact this had on Malcolm X and other African-American leaders was tremendous. With their long-lost brothers in Africa now free, American leaders were inspired to attempt what one writer called "the decolonization of the African American mind." [79] Like W.E.B. Du Bois and other Pan-Africanists before him, Malcolm hoped to rebridge the gap between Africans and African Americans, believing it could only benefit both to restore a sense of pride in their common ancestry. If American Jews could identify with the struggle of Jews in Israel, why shouldn't African Americans engage in dialogue with black Africans?

In April, Malcolm also traveled to Morocco, Algeria, Egypt, Sudan, Nigeria, and Ghana. At Accra, where Du Bois had died in exile the year before, Malcolm discovered an entire colony of African-American expatriates. Some had even renounced their American citizenship. He addressed the Ghanian Parliament and had an audience with President Kwame Nkrumah. At Ibadan University in Nigeria, Malcolm urged the newly independent African states to seek greater unity with their long-lost brothers in America and assist them, as a means of internationalizing the struggle, in indicting the United States on charges of racism before the United Nations.

Though some accused him of using Islam as a front, his travels to Africa and the Middle East were an attempt to discover the truth of Orthodox Islam, to broaden his perspective on the international context of black liberation, and to seek funding for the fledgling OAAU. Just as Malcolm Little had left prison reformed, in May, Malcolm X returned—bearded, goateed—to America as El-Hajj Malik El-Shabazz. In a news conference at Kennedy Airport, he pronounced himself a changed man. "In the past . . . I have been guilty of making sweeping indictments of *all* white people. I will never be guilty of that again . . . . The true Islam has shown me that a blanket indictment of all white people is as wrong as . . . blanket indictments against blacks." [80]

**ON HEALING**

Here I am, back in Mecca. I am still traveling, trying to broaden my mind, for I've seen too much of the damage narrow-mindedness can make of things, and when I return home to America, I will devote what energies I have to repairing the damage.

**Letter to James Farmer**

Malcolm speaks at one of the Sunday meetings of the Organization of Afro-American Unity in the Audubon Ballroom, December 1964.

# THE BALLOT OR THE BULLET

At 2:00 P.M., Malcolm drove to the Audubon Ballroom, where he had begun holding meetings each Sunday. His audience was non-Muslim now, though largely black. In his last days, Malcolm X was an organizer with neither coherent organization nor philosophy. Though he had been an effective mouthpiece for Elijah Muhammad, without the Nation behind him he was lost. His ideas were subject to change from month to month, speech to speech. He only knew he should reach out and be more open to cooperation and compromise, realizing that it would take people of all political, religious, economic, social, and even racial stripes to realize his vision.

Black nationalism no longer seemed synonymous with separatism. In a complete turnaround from Black Muslim doctrine, Malcolm came to believe that African Americans, whatever their grievance with whites, were Americans. For better or for worse, their destiny was tied to America, and they should stay and fight for what was theirs. At any rate, a return to Africa now seemed unrealistic. The enemy, he now saw, was not America but institutionalized racism. And broad-based political alliance—whites looking honestly, fearlessly within their hearts, and blacks taking greater responsibility for their actions and condition—seemed America's only hope.

He had to admit it: The NAACP was doing some good and had much in common with black nationalism. And while King preached nonviolence and civil disobedience, more militant factions such as SNCC and CORE began gaining political power. But Malcolm also saw that electoral politics alone could not cure the deep spiritual ills of African Americans. Hence the continuing need for some traditional religious affiliation. But how were blacks to get *civil* rights before they got their *human* rights? More ambitiously, he felt that if only African Americans would start thinking of themselves in international terms, they would see that they had a case for the United Nations on the grounds of human rights abuses.

Seeing that African Americans formed a majority in many communities, SNCC began coordinating voter registration drives in the Deep South during the 1964 presidential campaign. Malcolm finally saw the truth of what other leaders had been saying all along: With the white vote evenly divided between Republicans and Democrats, ten million black votes could decisively influence public policy on such increasingly critical issues as the Vietnam War. Malcolm likewise began encouraging voter registration, though between Lyndon Johnson and Barry Goldwater there seemed little choice. The one was a fox, the other a wolf. Goldwater, at least, was up-front about what he believed, and Malcolm respected that. But neither meant the black man any good. Malcolm warned—prophetically, as it turned out—that despite President-reelect Johnson's championing of the Civil Rights Act, the ghettos would explode unless deeper issues were addressed. America's choice was clear: the ballot or the bullet.

Malcolm knew he was a marked man. His house had been firebombed just the week before, and he had no insurance. He

---

**ON THE HUMAN FAMILY**

I believe in recognizing every human being as a human being, neither white, black, brown, nor red. When you are dealing with humanity as one family, there's no question of integration or intermarriage. It's just one human being marrying another human being or one human being living with another human being.

Interview with
Pierre Berton,
January 1965

Malcolm arrives at his home in Queens on February 14, 1965, after learning that the house has been firebombed.

didn't so much worry about himself, but he had a pregnant wife, children, a struggling organization, and one full-time employee to support. He was exhausted. His nerves were shot. Still, he felt that if he were going to do something, he should just make up his mind and do it without wavering or indecision.

To his dying day, Malcolm regretted his lack of formal education. He could easily have spent his entire life far from the struggle, just reading and thinking. There were so many interests he might have pursued: history, religion, law, languages. He would have liked to have a working knowledge of Arabic, of course. And Chinese—now there was a language to learn. *That* was the language of the future. If only there had been more time....

At 2:30, since he had ordered that there be no weapons searches at the door, Malcolm scanned the audience for  Fruit of Islam renegades from Temple No. 7. "*Salaam Alaikum,*" he began. "Get your hand out of my pocket!"[81] someone shouted. A smoke bomb went off in the back of the room. Malcolm urged calm. As his bodyguards rushed from his side and into the audience, a man in the front row pulled a sawed-off shotgun from under his coat, unloading it into Malcolm's chest.

"They're killing my husband!" Betty screamed. Malcolm fell to the floor. At least two more gunmen ran up from the front rows to the stage where he lay dying. Firing repeatedly into his body, they dashed for the exits as an audience of four hundred scrambled in both panic and outraged pursuit. One assassin was wounded by the mob and captured just as a squad car arrived. Someone gave Malcolm mouth-to-mouth resuscitation, but it was too late. He was placed on a stretcher and rushed to nearby Columbia-Presbyterian Hospital. And at 3:30 P.M. on February 21, 1965, Malcolm X was pronounced dead.

Years later, at Attica, convicted killer Thomas Hagan swore out an affidavit stating that Norman 3X Butler and Thomas 15X Johnson, two of the alleged assassins also sentenced to life in prison, had in fact been framed. And though, unlike him, they

**Malcolm is taken on a stretcher after the fatal shooting in the Audubon Ballroom on February 21, 1965.**

were eventually paroled, Hagan refused to reveal the real conspirators' names. Subsequent motions for retrial have been stonewalled by federal and state authorities.

Framed? By whom? And why? Both Butler and Johnson were members of the Temple No. 7 Fruit of Islam, which put them under immediate suspicion of retaliating against Malcolm for the defamation of the Honorable Elijah Muhammad. Was Hagan, as the prosecutor claimed, merely the fall guy? Or was he telling the truth?

Why had Malcolm failed to inform the police of threats upon his life? Because, he had shrugged, "they know it already." [82] He had applied for a gun permit, presumably for self-defense, but the application was still pending. In spite of the fact that he was in obvious danger, there were no uniformed policemen on the scene that day. But unknown to Malcolm's security, two undercover policemen were stationed offstage, and there was even an FBI agent in the audience, who later filed a report confirming that four black males had indeed been involved in the assassination.

The FBI declined to pursue an official investigation, saying it was a routine murder case, a matter for the local police. Recent information from FBI files indicates that Director J. Edgar Hoover, in his anxiety over the rise of a militant "black Messiah," masterminded a counterintelligence operation known as Cointelpro. Through its strategically located Chicago office, the bureau coordinated a systematic campaign to discredit the Nation of Islam and other so-called radical groups. Preventing potential alliances by setting faction against faction and even provoking outright war within ranks, the FBI played a deadly game of divide-and-conquer.

Theories about the death of Malcolm X abound. Some—proposed mostly by members of the Nation—link the FBI directly to the assassination. A more moderate stance puts the FBI in an indirect role, as the organization that set up the kill. The most accepted theory implicates the Black Muslims as the assassins. However, even though many people find an assassination order from within the organization conceivable, they are more skeptical of the Nation's ability to manage the cover-up without outside help.

The facts, however inconclusive or circumstantial, are the following. Malcolm's telephone—like Martin's—was wire-tapped, and a conversation between them about how best to proceed with civil rights strategy was recorded just before Malcolm's house was firebombed. Malcolm was led to believe that his death had indeed been ordered by Elijah Muhammad.

Who was ultimately responsible for the murder of Malcolm X? The questions are clear. The answers we may never know.

Women mourn the loss
of their spokesman,
Malcolm X, as his body
is carried from Harlem's
Faith Temple where
funeral services were
held. One thousand
people attended.

**AFTERWORD**

Traditionally, Black Muslim funerals were brief. The minister would read a short prayer over the casket, followed by an obituary notice. There were to be no tears, no wailing, no flowers. Those were for the living, not the dead. Besides, any money spent on such spectacles was better off donated to the family. Accordingly, trays were passed around for collection, and disks of peppermint candy handed out. At the minister's cue, these were inserted in the mouth as the mourners filed quietly by for one last look. Like candy dissolving gradually, sweetly, so should the departed pass into memory.

Malcolm's funeral took place a week after his assassination, at the Faith Temple Church of God in Christ. Six hundred mourners crowded inside. Outside in the bitter cold huddled thousands more—shocked, grieved, relieved, or merely numb. For a few, both black and white, Malcolm had been a nuisance they wished would go away. For many others, he was a show of rhetorical force such as they had never witnessed, someone who filled them with pride, making them feel for the first time in their lives no longer ashamed of being black. It was as if, when Malcolm X was murdered, something in them had been assassinated, too.

His death marked a wave of revolt in American cities that began with Watts in 1965 and came full circle with South

**ON EARTHLY REWARDS**

Whenever I walk the street and see people ready to get with it, that's my reward.

Interview with Claude Lewis, December 1964

Central Los Angeles in 1992. Despite decades of social, political, and economic progress, blacks remained overrepresented in prisons and on playing fields and underrepresented in classrooms and boardrooms. Between despair in the ghettos and fear in the suburbs, the consensus still seemed that the situation was hopeless. The two nations remained, to still too great an extent, separate and unequal.

A generation after his death, Malcolm had "come to mean more than himself," as one writer put it, his stature deriving "as much from his detractors' exaggerated fears as from his admirers' exalted hopes." [83] Many factions began laying claim to Malcolm X, which hadn't always been the case. Amiri Baraka (Leroi Jones) recalled giving an address at Howard University the year of Malcolm's assassination and being booed for merely mentioning his name. His life and words have been well documented. But the sudden resurgence of popular interest in Malcolm X during the nineties, after a generation of relative neglect, begs other questions: Who was Malcolm X? What was Malcolm X?

*Webster's Dictionary* identifies him as an "American civil rights leader." His assistant minister, who was "as close as anybody could get to him without burning up," said it "was impossible to really know him." [84] Yet, almost everyone had fixed ideas about Malcolm X—everyone, that is, but Malcolm. An enigma in life, in death he became a symbol, which ensured he would be remembered. But not even Malcolm could have imagined what he ultimately became: brand "X," a fashion statement worn on baseball caps and T-shirts, the subject of books, pictures, videos, operas, and movie epics. Rich if not discriminating, popular culture has conferred upon him a cult status based almost entirely on images, catch phrases, and snippets of speeches rather than a cool examination of his thought.

Not perhaps since Marcus Garvey has a black leader so completely captured the popular imagination. What was the reason for Malcolm's sudden reemergence, particularly among young people born long after his death? Was it a response to the waning influence of the civil rights movement and the Nation of Islam after Elijah Muhammad's death in 1975? Or the lack of charismatic political leadership during the seventies and eighties? Malcolm had long appealed to artists and intellectuals, who admired him for saying what others knew but were either unable or else unwilling to say. He remained one of the founding fathers of black nationalism, a prophet of the Black Power movement, and a source of inspiration for the new Afrocentricism in scholarship, dress, and hairstyles. But the middle classes despised and feared him. He "kept snatching our lies away," said Ossie Davis. "He kept shouting the painful truth we . . . did not want to hear . . . . And he would not stop for love or money." [85]

There were two Malcolms: pre- and post-Mecca. Where Martin Luther King was all transcendence and Christian forgiveness, until Mecca, Malcolm seemed consumed with anger and hatred. But, during the nineties, he seemed to speak most urgently to the disenfranchised whom King had failed to reach. According to the mythology of this gangster chic, he was resurrected Public Enemy No. 1, patron saint of hip-hop, at once uncompromisingly militant and widely popular, an angry icon of black rage who became a best-seller for his very refusal to sell out. Shotgun at the ready, defending his turf "by any means necessary," Malcolm X became the rebel with a cause, a hero who "lived fast and died young," going out "in a blaze of glory." [86] Youth tends to equate revolution with rebellion, not with the profound and lasting change of patient reform. Lusting after the glamorous potency of the twelve-gauge while neglecting the more mundane realities of adulthood, would-be gangsters look up to Malcolm X with precisely the sort of misguided hero-worship he once held for Harlem mobsters. Malcolm understood discontent, but he also worked hard to defeat the ignorance by which he knew himself to be imprisoned. If he had not broken free of the streets, he would never have become a hero to the discontented.

**From a mural on the walls of the Audubon Ballroom. Images tell the story of the ongoing struggle for blacks to claim their rightful place in American society.**

A man of action dead at thirty-nine, Malcolm X lived twice the average life in half the average lifetime. If anything, a generation has proved ample time to show that the less than twenty years from his religious conversion to his death, with all the stops and starts between, was simply too little time for him to hammer out a coherent philosophy. The bookish activist left behind mere "fragments of political speech, not systematic social thought; suggestive ideological gestures more than substantive political activity." [87]

His life, like his *Autobiography,* is a classic narrative of transformation and redemption. For better and for worse, in public and on the record, Malcolm X made himself up as he went along. He took chances. He made mistakes. The consequence of his willingness to change was that people never quite knew what to believe. In the life of Malcolm X, as in all our lives, change was the only constant. His legacy is less a conclusion than a search. And, ultimately, it was his determination to continue searching at all costs that ensured his salvation.

What John Brown had been to the abolitionist movement a century before, Malcolm X was to the civil rights movement: part folk hero, part fool, part saint. If his wisdom was sometimes doubtful, his bravery was never in question. No less than that of Martin Luther King or any of the other sanctified figures of the civil rights era, the memory of Malcolm X is part of the national legacy.

"For the freedom of my . . . 22 million black brothers and sisters here in America, I do believe that I have fought the best that I knew how, and the best I could, with the shortcomings that I have had."[88] Malcolm X believed that one day history might show that his words, bitter as they seemed, were what the nation needed to wake it from complacency or even disaster. "If I can die having brought any light, having exposed any meaningful truth . . . then all of the credit is due to Allah. Only the mistakes have been mine."[89]

**ON RACISM**

**Once I was, yes. But now I have turned my direction away from anything that's racist.**

**Interview with Robert Penn Warren, 1964**

| | |
|---|---|
| 1925 | Born in Omaha, Nebraska, May 19 |
| 1940 | Moves to Boston |
| 1941-1946 | Small-time hustler in Harlem |
| 1946 | Arrested for burglary, sentenced to ten years in prison |
| 1947-1952 | Introduced to Islam, converts |
| 1952 | Released from prison, joins Nation of Islam, becoming minister |
| 1957 | Founds influential Black Muslim publication *Muhammad Speaks* |
| 1959 | Broadcast documentary "The Hate that Hate Produced" and C. Eric Lincoln's *Black Muslims in America* appear |
| 1963 | With Alex Haley, begins collaboration on *The Autobiography of Malcolm X*; President John F. Kennedy assassinated |
| 1964 | Breaks with Elijah Muhammad and the Nation of Islam; founds the Muslim Mosque, Inc., and later the Organization of Afro-American Unity; makes pilgrimage to Mecca |
| 1965 | Assassinated February 21 at the Audubon Ballroom in New York City |

*Books*

Breitman, George. *Assassination of Malcolm X.* New York: Pathfinder, 1991.

———————. *Malcolm X Speaks: Selected Speeches and Statements.* New York: Grove Weidenfeld, 1990.

Carson, Clayborne. *Malcolm X: The FBI File.* New York: Carroll & Graf, 1991.

Clark, Kenneth. *King, Malcolm, Baldwin: Three Interviews.* Scranton, Pa.: University Press of New England, 1985.

Davis, Lenwood G. *Malcolm X: A Selected Bibliography.* Westport, Conn.: Greenwood Publishing Group, 1984.

Davis, Thulani. *Malcolm X: The Great Photographs.* New York: Stewart Tabori & Chang, 1992.

Doctor, Bernard A. *Malcolm X for Beginners.* New York: Writers & Readers Publishing, 1992.

Epps, Archie. *Malcolm X: Speeches at Harvard.* New York: Paragon House, 1991.

Essien-Udom, E. U. *Black Nationalism: A Search for an Identity in America.* University of Chicago Press, 1962.

Gallen, David. *Malcolm X As They Knew Him.* New York: Carroll & Graf, 1992.

———————. *Malcolm A to X: The Man and His Ideas.* New York: Carroll & Graf, 1992.

Haley, Alex. *The Autobiography of Malcolm X.* New York: Ballantine, 1965.

Haskins, Jim. *I Have a Dream: The Life and Words of Martin Luther King, Jr.* Brookfield, Conn.: The Millbrook Press, 1992.

Johnson, Timothy V. *Malcolm X: A Comprehensive Annotated Bibliography.* New York: Garland Publishing, 1986.

Karim, Imam Benjamin. *The End of White World Supremacy: Four Speeches by Malcolm X.* New York: Arcade/Little, Brown, 1971.

Lincoln, C. Eric. *The Black Muslims in America.* New York: Kayode, 1991.

Marable, Manning. *The Malcolm X Reader: His Life, His Thought, His Legacy.* New York: New American Library, 1993.

Perry, Bruce. *Malcolm X: The Last Speeches*. New York: Pathfinder Press, 1989.

Wood, Joe. *Malcolm X: In Our Own Image.* New York: St. Martin's, 1992.


*Articles, Speeches, Broadcasts, and Videos*

Baldwin, James. "Malcolm and Martin," *Esquire*, April 1972.

Dyson, Michael Eric. "Who Speaks for Malcolm X?" *The New York Times Book Review,* November 29, 1992, pp. 3, 29–33.

Fayer, Steve, and Bagwell, Orlando. "The American Experience/Malcolm X: Make it Plain," Blackside Inc./ROJA Productions Inc., 1994.

Frady, Marshall. "The Children of Malcolm," *The New Yorker*, October 12, 1992, pp. 64–72.

Gates, Henry Louis. "Malcolm, the Aardvark and Me," *The New York Times Book Review*, February 21, 1993, p. 11.

Haley, Alex. Interview, *Playboy*, May 1963.

Kunstler, William M. "The Real Murderers of Malcolm X," *Shadow* #28, December 1992/May 1993, pp. 6, 8–9, 14.

Lee, Spike, director. *Malcolm X*, 1992.

Mueller, Dennis, and Ellis, Deb. "FBI's War on Black America," MPI Home Video, 1990.

Wallace, Mike, and Lomax, Louis. "The Hate that Hate Produced," *Newsbeat*. New York: WNTA-TV, July 10, 1959.

X, Malcolm. "Message to the Grass Roots." Afro-American Broadcasting and Recording Company.

**NOTES**

1. Quoted in Joe Wood, ed., *Malcolm X: In Our Own Image* (New York: St. Martin's, 1992), p. 488.
2. Wood, p. 56.
3. Quoted in David Gallen, ed., *Malcolm A to X: The Man and His Ideas* (New York: Carroll & Graf, 1992), p. 91.
4. Alex Haley, *The Autobiography of Malcolm X* (New York: Ballantine, 1965), p. 1.
5. Haley, p. 378.
6. Haley, p. 7.
7. Haley, p. 4
8. Haley, p. 6.
9. Ibid.
10. Haley, p. 3.
11. Haley, p. 12.
12. Haley, p. 18.
13. Haley, p. 40.
14. Haley, p. 76.
15. Haley, p. 73.
16. Haley, p. 121.
17. Haley, p. 91.
18. Haley, p. 138.
19. Haley, p. 134.
20. Haley, p. 143.
21. Ibid.
22. Haley, p. 155.
23. Haley, p. 134.
24. Ibid.

25. Haley, p. 164.
26. Haley, p. 170.
27. Haley, p. 179.
28. Haley, p. 173.
29. Haley, p. 185.
30. Haley, p. 197.
31. Haley, p. 198.
32. Haley, p. 199.
33. Haley, p. 210.
34. Marshall Frady, "The Children of Malcolm" (*The New Yorker*, October 12, 1992), p. 64.
35. Haley, p. 233.
36. Haley, p. 215.
37. C. Eric Lincoln, *The Black Muslims in America* (New York: Kayode, 1991), p. 138.
38. Lincoln, p. 99.
39. Haley, p. 269.
40. Haley, p. 241.
41. Haley, p. 394.
42. Lincoln, p. 156.
43. Haley, p. 265.
44. Haley, p. 39.
45. Haley, p. 197.
46. Lincoln, p. 101.
47. Frady, p. 70.
48. Haley, p. 242.
49. Haley, p. 417.
50. Frady, p. 72.
51. George Breitman, *Malcolm X Speaks: Selected Speeches and Statements* (New York: Grove Weidenfeld, 1990), p. 25.
52. Jim Haskins, *I Have a Dream: The Life and Words of Martin Luther King, Jr.* (Brookfield, Conn.: The Millbrook Press, 1992), p. 51.
53. Haley, p. 278.
54. Michael Eric Dyson, "Who Speaks for Malcolm X?" (*The New York Times Book Review,* November 29, 1992), p. 31.
55. Frady, p. 66.
56. Haley, p. 374.

57. Wood, p. 26.
58. Haley, p. 285
59. Breitman, p. 45.
60. Haley, p. 393.
61. Haley, p. 266.
62. Haley, p. 318.
63. Haley, p. 319.
64. Haley, p. 142.
65. Haley, p. 302.
66. Gallen, p. 138.
67. Haley, p. 429.
68. Frady, p. 72.
69. Haley, p. 304.
70. Haley, p. 306.
71. Haley, p. 296.
72. Haley, p. 210.
73. Frady, p. 72.
74. Haley, p. 305.
75. Gallen, p. 48.
76. Haley, p. 374.
77. Gallen, p. 105.
78. Haley, p. 323.
79. Dyson, p. 3.
80. Gallen, p. 34.
81. Haley, p. 362.
82. William M. Kunstler, "The Real Murderers of Malcolm X" (*Shadow* #28, December 1992/May 1993), p. 6.
83. Lincoln, p. 211.
84. Dyson, p. 29.
85. Frady, p. 69.
86. Haley, p. 458.
87. Wood, p. 185.
88. Dyson, p. 30.
89. Haley, p. 379.

# INDEX